NO ORDINARY PREY

By Nelson Naicker

A wholly owned subsidiary of TBN

DEDICATION

I am dedicating this book to my parents, Sunny and Salome Naicker. Through their lives, in the lessons they taught, and in their example, they modeled a "No Ordinary Prey" lifestyle and attitude. They never let circumstances, other people, or challenges deter them from being who God wanted them to be and from doing what needed to be done for the kingdom of God.

My dad had lung cancer, and he passed away on August 10, 2015. It has been a painful challenge for our family. My dad did something so incredible on the day that he learned that he had a tumor in his lung. After a long day of medical tests and meetings with the doctor, my dad came home and promptly went to deliver bread, cakes, and rolls to the poor in the community. His passion was to care for the poor. For many years, he led the feeding program at his church until it was closed down. However, it did not stop him from personally reaching out to feed the poor. On this dark day in our family's history, my dad was about God's kingdom business. When I spoke to him later that day and asked him why he was not home resting, his response was this, "People are in need, and I have a job to do." That line will always stay with me.

That attitude is a "No Ordinary Prey" response. That is the theme of this book. In the months that followed, my dad had to deal with unbearable pain, radiation and chemotherapy, and a host of medications, yet he continued to wake up in the early hours of the morning to keep his morning prayer appointment with the Lord.

ACKNOWLEDGMENTS

I would like to express my thanks to my family. I am grateful for the love and support of my wife, Valerie, and our children, Kimberly and Jordan. There are not enough words to express how much I appreciate your unconditional love and support during my Seminary years and your willingness to go where the ministry took us. Through it all, we ended up having so many wonderful adventures.

I am also grateful to my sister, Vanessa, for her support and for the amazing way she has taken care of our parents. And I also want to express my thanks to my sister's husband, Devian, my in-laws, and our extended family for their prayers.

I thank God for the El Bethel Assembly of God Church family in Staten Island, New York. Your prayers and your love and support for my family and me have provided the opportunity for us to grow in the ministry. I most especially would like to thank Peter Lisi. It was his encouragement that got me to finally finish this manuscript, and his help directed me to Trilogy Publishing. He is largely responsible for this book being in your hands.

I want to thank Tricia Horn, Jennifer Hudson, the editors at WorldMissionMedia, and the Trilogy Publishing team for all their help.

TABLE OF CONTENTS

INTRODUCTION

Eric Nerhus, an Australian professional diver, made the headlines several years ago. His specialty was abalone, a type of shellfish. He did not use scuba gear, just an air hose. He tells his story that on a day like any other day, he was out diving on the Australian coast while his son was in the boat. He was in a spot where he had dived hundreds of times before. Suddenly he was engulfed with blackness, and he felt himself being shaken from side to side, and he immediately knew that he was being attacked by a shark.

His upper torso was in the shark's mouth. Being an experienced diver, he knew that he needed to stay calm in emergencies. He remembered his training and tried to gouge out the eyes of the shark. That was impossible, but it did cause an irritation in the eye of the shark, which caused the shark to loosen its grip, so he wriggled free.

The shark circled him a few times and left. Eric Nerhus got away and lived to tell his story. When he broke free, the shark circled him, and Eric said (*I paraphrase*), "The shark must have been thinking, *This is not my usual prey...not part of the regular food chain.*" There were dolphins and seals in the area, and they were what the shark fed on. When a shark bites into a seal, it feels flesh, blubber, or soft meat. But when the shark bit into him, it hit metal from the diving gear because he had on his lead-weighted jacket. Then he fought back in a way that a seal or dolphin could not do. All of these things may have caused the shark to "think" this was not its usual prey.

The moment I heard his story, it stirred something in my spirit. That comment he made regarding his survival became the basis for a yearly ministry theme, a sermon series, and for this book, *No Ordinary Prey*.

It means even more to me because I was born a victim. I was born and raised in South Africa under the Apartheid regime. And we suffered the injustices of this system until democracy was established under Nelson Mandela in 1994.

Born a victim. I lived as a victim. Even more—I had the mentality of a victim. And this dominated my thinking for many years. God does not want us living as powerless victims. We often end up being victims of life, circumstances, even other people, and the devil. God wants us to fight back. God has empowered us to fight back. We are no ordinary prey for the devil.

The Enemy of Our Souls

We have trouble in the world. The causes of the troubles are that this is a fallen world, and the sin of Adam and Eve continues to cause problems with our natural world. We have trouble because of people. And often, we are the manufacturers of our own trouble. The biggest troublemaker in our lives is the devil. He is "the enemy of our souls." John 10:10 (NIV) says, "The thief comes only in order to steal and kill and destroy." First Peter 5:8 (NIV) warns, "Your enemy the devil prowls around like a roaring lion looking for someone to devour." Satan is always on the lookout for ways to destroy us.

The devil knows our history, so he attacks our historically weak areas. He wants to destroy our lives, our health, our marriages, our families. He especially targets our faith and our God-given destiny.

This is the foundational statement for this book—every time the devil attacks us, he needs to know that we are not his "usual prey" because of the way we respond and because of the way we fight back. More importantly, because of who we belong to. First John 4:4 (NIV) declares, "...the one who is in you is greater than the one who is in the world." No ordinary prey.

The devil made a mistake in letting Daniel step into the den of lions. He should have killed the lions because the outcome of that attack brought a change in the laws for that nation (Daniel 6:21–28). The devil made a mistake putting the Hebrew young men, Shadrach, Meshach, and Abednego, into the fiery furnace because that demonic agenda resulted in Nebuchadnezzar having a vision of God and changing the laws (Daniel 3:24–30). The devil made a serious error in judgment when he plotted to destroy Mordechai, Esther, and their people. God turned it around on their enemies (Esther 8:7–17). The devil made a mistake putting Paul and Silas in prison because God broke their chains, and the jailer and his family were saved (Acts 16). The devil messed up in targeting Job because God gave him double for his trouble (Job 42).

The best example of all is that the devil made the biggest mistake by inciting the Jews to crucify Jesus! We all know how that turned out! Jesus rose from the dead and destroyed death, hell, and the grave! And today, we have salvation and eternal life in Jesus Christ.

We are no ordinary prey. Whatever attack comes against you, realize that God can turn it around. We have to stop seeing the attack of the devil as failure or that we are losing the battle. Instead, see it as an opportunity to reverse that attack back on the devil and the forces of hell. See it as a moment for God to get the glory through our lives. Hallelujah! Let the devil know that he made a mistake when he set his sights on you because God is going to boomerang that attack back on him.

CHAPTER ONE
Thought Bumpers

When our children were little, they used the bumpers when we went bowling. The bumpers would prevent the ball from ending up in the gutters. That gave me the excuse to do the same. But as our children got older, they no longer wanted to bowl with the bumpers. On the other hand, I could not bowl without the bumpers. Just as in bowling, we need "thought bumpers" to stop the devil from pulling our thoughts, imaginations, and emotions into the "gutter" of fear and intimidation.

Allow these verses that I am going to share with you to serve as thought bumpers. There are many ways that the devil can trip us up. These powerful promises act as safeguards against us accepting the lies that we are powerless victims in the spiritual warfare.

Before I share some lessons on how we can fight back against the devil, let me remind you of a foundational principle in spiritual warfare—when Jesus Christ is our Lord and Savior, we are undefeatable. Before you think this is nonsense and choose to stop reading any further, allow me to back up this claim with the Word of God. We have some awesome promises related to the spiritual warfare.

Promise #1

"No weapon forged against you will prevail, and you will refute every tongue that accuses you. This is the heritage of the servants of the LORD, and this is their vindication from me," declares the LORD.

— Isaiah 54:17 (NIV)

What a powerful promise. No weapon formed against us will prosper. The Hebrew word is *ṣālēa*. That means it will not prosper, will not succeed, and will not progress. In other words, an attack may be launched, but it will not achieve or accomplish its assignment.

Today you may be under attack. God's promise to you is that the thing coming against you has an expiry date. God is saying to us, "Before you know it, that attack will disintegrate, diminish, and disappear." Hallelujah! That is so worthy of a praise dance!

You may feel like you are losing, but hold on to God. It is the end result that matters, and God says you will win!

Promise #2

"And I tell you that you are Peter, and on this rock I will build my church, and the gates of Hades will not overcome it."

— Matthew 16:18 (NIV)

Jesus gave a powerful promise to the disciples and to His church. The Greek word is *katischyō*. That means it will not overcome or overpower. Further, it will not be stronger than or superior in strength to the church.

What a powerful promise. Please allow that promise to sink deep into your soul. The devil will never be stronger than the church. Why? Because Jesus said so. Whatever you are fighting against, you are greater than that attack. Catch this—Christian, you are not the weaker one in the battle!

Promise #3

…This is what the LORD says to you: "Do not be afraid or discouraged because of this vast army. For the battle is not yours, but God's."

— 2 Chronicles 20:15 (NIV)

We all love this verse. It is the favorite verse for many Christians. This is a powerful verse. God is fighting for us. You may be facing a battle with overwhelming odds against you. But do not give up because the Lord God Almighty is about to step in and conquer your enemies. God has never lost a battle, and He never will.

Promise #4

"If you listen carefully to what he says and do all that I say, I will be an enemy to your enemies and will oppose those who oppose you."

— Exodus 23:22 (NIV)

This is a wow verse. It does not even need an explanation. The Hebrew word *ʾāyaḇ* means "to treat as an enemy or to be hostile towards." The second Hebrew word is *ṣûr*. That word means "to bind, besiege, confine, cramp, and to secure, shut in, or shut up."

We are winners because God is on our side! That means anything that comes against you to destroy you just made itself an enemy of God!

This person, the thing, or the demon that came against you just made the biggest mistake of their existence. This promise means that you are not alone in this battle, and you are not a powerless victim or without hope.

These are just a few of numerous verses in the Bible that speak about our victory in the spiritual warfare. Many of us are familiar with the verses that speak about us being "the head and not the tail," "above and not beneath," verses that say we are "overcomers," "more than conquerors," and "triumphant in Christ."

Let these promises guard your heart and mind when you find yourself in a spiritual battle. Unless we have these "bumpers," the devil will weaken us with his lies. And many of us struggle with vain imaginations, fear, and anxiety. We accept defeat without even knowing what is rightfully ours in Christ Jesus. It is time for the Christians to be educated about those blessings that are rightfully ours because of the blood of Jesus Christ.

My goal in this book is not to introduce some new doctrine about spiritual warfare. Neither is it to give you ten steps to instant victory. But rather to remind you of what is rightfully yours as the people of God. This is to encourage you to put into practice what you may have heard and already believe.

CHAPTER TWO
Don't Accept Defeat

When Valerie was a little girl, the doctors had given her mom, Gonum Hyman, just weeks to live. But God miraculously healed her of cancer. She was instantly and completely healed! Of course, her doctors could not medically explain what had happened.

My mother-in-law boldly shared her story with everyone and anyone. She grabbed every opportunity to share her testimony and to pray with people. Because of her testimony and her prayers, almost everyone in her family became Christians. Most of them were more than just churchgoers; they became fully committed followers of Jesus. And today, a few nephews are pastoring a church. And many of their family friends were saved because of her story. She spent many hours praying over people on the phone; she would even pray over people in the stores; her doctors and several pastors came to her for prayer.

She was a warrior, and she never backed down from a fight. She had other health issues over the years, but she did not let that stop her. She pushed through in her prayers, and God healed her over and over again. And that was her encouragement to everyone she met to never give up because of our God. Through her prayers, the sick were healed, barren women had children, and people were delivered and blessed.

And she continued with such fervency to witness and to pray over people all the days of her life. Valerie's mom never accepted defeat. She always fought back against the attacks of the devil. She passed away in 2020, but her legacy still continues.

Context

Most of us know the story of Job. A quick recap is that Job had lost all his possessions one after another after another. All his children died on the same day in the same place, in one moment. Then Job lost his health, and his entire body was covered with boils.

We do not fully understand why this good man suffered. There are no easy answers. His losses are common to humanity. Financial setbacks happen as people do lose everything and end up bankrupt. Some people bury their children. Others get sick with cancer, AIDS, hepatitis B, and other chronic illnesses. People lose the support of their spouse; the divorce statistics tell the story. People do lose their reputation in the community. Others lose friends; people are deserted or betrayed by their friends.

It was the intensity of the attacks against Job that made his experience unusual. They happened in quick succession. While the first messenger was speaking, another one appeared on the scene with the next bad report, and while he was talking, the next messenger came. It was one devastating blow after another after another. A person would have to live very long and have a very hard life to experience what Job went through. Job had all that packed into a very short space of time. Bible scholars believe that this happened within a nine-month period.

> When Job's three friends, Eliphaz… Bildad… and
> Zophar… set out from their homes… to go and
> sympathize with him and comfort him.

When they saw him from a distance, they could
hardly recognize him; they began to weep aloud,
and they tore their robes and sprinkled dust on their
heads. Then they sat on the ground with him for
seven days and seven nights. No one said a word to
him, because they saw how great his suffering was.

— Job 2:11–13 (NIV)

This man was so knocked out of shape that his own friends
could not recognize him. When your friends cannot recognize
you, that says a lot about the state you are in. They were so stunned
that they wept aloud. He was broken beyond recognition.

Here are a few verses that explain the extent of his suffering.

"I have become a laughingstock to my friends…"

— Job 12:4 (NIV)

Friends are supposed to be our defenders. When your friends
mock you and laugh at your pain, that is a very deep wound.

Then Job replied: "I have heard many things like
these; you are miserable comforters, all of you!"

— Job 16:1–2 (NIV)

"To comfort" means "to console and to be moved with pity
and compassion." The Hebrew word used here is *amal*. That means
"troublesome." These friends were just making matters worse.

"My relatives have gone away; my closest friends
have forgotten me."

— Job 19:14 (NIV)

Job also suffers alienation from his family and his friends.

> "I summon my servant, but he does not answer,
> though I beg him with my own mouth."
>
> — Job 19:16 (NIV)

Job struggled with disrespect from his own servants.

> "My breath is offensive to my wife; I am loathsome
> to my own family."
>
> — Job 19:17 (NIV)

And then there is the intimate disconnection. Even his wife could not stand to be near him. And even his own family could not be near him.

> "Even the little boys scorn me; when I appear, they
> ridicule me."
>
> — Job 19:18 (NIV)

Job was respected by the men and the elders of the town prior to his setbacks. Now even little kids were making fun of him.

> "All my intimate friends detest me; those I love have
> turned against me."
>
> — Job 19:19 (NIV)

This statement sums it up well.

> His wife said to him, "Are you still maintaining your
> integrity? Curse God and die!"
>
> — Job 2:9 (NIV)

Here is the biggest blow. His own wife attacks his faith and his integrity. "Curse God and die." Was she ready for him to die? Maybe she blamed him for the loss of their children. It is one thing to lose everything, but something totally different is to lose the support of your spouse. It is one thing to lose people's respect and support, but it is a different level of betrayal when it happens in your own home. Now Job was all alone.

Job's wife's words are recorded only once. And it is probably one of the most ungodly, vile, despicable words ever uttered in the Bible.

At the start of chapter 23, Job is saying that he cannot reach God. It seems like God is not reachable to him. He says, "I go in all directions, and I cannot find God." We get the sense that he feels like he is unheard and unseen. We can sense the utter loneliness of the man. He is broken beyond measure. And you thought you were having a bad day.

Potential Gaps

I want to add different angles to the story today. You don't have to agree, but I just want you to think about this too.

Clarify the Confession

"[Job said] The LORD gave and the LORD has taken away; may the name of the LORD be praised."
— Job 1:21 (NIV)

Let's be clear; God does not play games with people. God does not give blessings and then take them away. Job makes that confession, but we see it from a different angle because we have information that Job does not and because we know that it was the devil that took from him.

We know that Job did not blame God. He didn't blame anyone else. He did not blame the enemies, nor did he blame the weather. Here is a suggestion; Job's confession was an acknowledgment that everything belongs to God. And if God took it, that was fine because Job would still worship Him with or without the stuff.

Children

> His sons used to hold feasts in their homes on their
> birthdays, and they would invite their three sisters to
> eat and drink with them. When a period of feasting
> had run its course, Job would make arrangements for
> them to be purified. Early in the morning he would
> sacrifice a burnt offering for each of them, think-
> ing, "Perhaps my children have sinned and cursed
> God in their hearts." This was Job's regular custom.
> — Job 1:4–5 (NIV)

Have you ever asked yourself why he prayed this way? Why did Job feel this way? Have you ever prayed that way but did not have concrete evidence that something was not right in someone's life? But you felt the need to pray and ask God to have mercy in case something was a little off. Job was a man of God, and he may have had some discernment that his kids were not on the straight and narrow path. The other question is this: Why wasn't Job invited, or did he turn down the invitation? Was he excluded because they did not want him to see what they were doing? Job was praying for their forgiveness every time they had a party.

Here is something to think about. God didn't just let his children die just so he could replace them with better ones. Children are not like cell phones or cars; you don't just upgrade them with new ones every few years.

There may have been a reason his children perished that we don't know about. But Job's practice gives us a glimpse. Job felt that all was not well with his sons and daughters.

Wife

His wife said… "Curse God and die!"

— Job 2:9 (NIV)

Here is what the devil said to God.

"But now stretch out your hand and strike everything he has, and he will surely curse you to your face."

— Job 1:11 (NIV)

Did you catch the words of the wife and how they matched those of Satan? She was living under his roof and may not have been fully committed to God. Isn't it amazing that the wife is not attacked? Meanwhile, the sons and daughters died, and all the possessions were destroyed, and Job's health crashed. Makes you think, doesn't it?

Fear

"What I feared has come upon me; what I dread-
ed has happened to me."

— Job 3:25 (NIV)

There are various explanations for this verse. Was this fear there
before the trials came upon Job? Or did this fear arise as a result
of his trials? Does this offer us a glimpse into Job's trials? Did fear
open the door for the devil to do what he did? Was Job saying
that he was obsessed with losing everything and everyone?

Job is considered one of the oldest books in the Bible. It is
believed that he lived sometime just after Noah's flood and before
Abraham's calling. He is generally placed in the Genesis chapter
10 to chapter 11 period.

I said all that to make this point—Job was a godly man, but
his life was not perfect before the attack of the devil. He has some
stuff going on, just like everyone else. It is my opinion and my belief that God did not use Job as a target practice. It is my opinion
and my belief that God did not put Job through all that suffering
just so that He could say to the devil, "Told you so." God does not
need to prove Himself to the devil. God does not need to prove
that He is telling the truth. God is God. And He is secure in being God. God does not turn a life upside to prove a point. It does
not match the nature and character of our God. God put a mark
on Cain so that no one would kill Cain. The God who went to the
cross for us does not play games with people just for the fun of it.
There is a lot more to the story of Job than we know. One more
thought. Did you notice that we never hear about Satan after the
early part of chapter two, and there are still forty more chapters
in the book?

But the bottom line and key lesson is that Job stayed faithful to God despite horrific attacks against him.

> "But he knows the way that I take; when he has tested me, I will come forth as gold."
>
> — Job 23:10 (NIV)

Gold After the Fire

Job was talking about gold going through the fire. We know that gold has to be mined because it is found underground in the form of rock. There is not much that we can do with a lump of gold until it goes through the fire. Fire removes the impurities. Fire makes it malleable, so it can be shaped into different forms. After it has been through the fire, gold can be turned into jewelry. And after the fire, gold is more attractive, more desired. After the fire, gold is more valuable and more useful or usable.

Job was saying this, "I will come through this trial like gold through the fire." That is a very strong statement. After all that just happened to Job, he was making this declaration, "When this is over, I will be better"; he was saying, "When this is over, I will be stronger and wiser." Job announced, "When this trial is over, I will know more, and I will understand more, and I will have more and be more. In other words, I will be at a higher level."

This Job said, "I am going to be okay, and actually, I am going to be more than okay because I am coming out of this better than before." If we did not know the end of the story, we would say, "Lock him up and throw away the key because he has lost his mind." Everything just went up in flames. He lost everything, and even his wife said, "Accept defeat and die." But Job refused.

Job not only expected to survive what he was going through; he expected to be better because of it.

He said some other radical statements.

"I know that my redeemer lives…"
— Job 19:25 (NIV)

A redeemer is a rescuer, savior, or liberator. Job's confession was, "I am in a mess, but my Savior is alive, and He is coming for me. It may not look like it, but I know in my heart and my mind that everything is going to be okay."

"Though He slay me, yet will I [trust] in Him…"
— Job 13:15 (NIV)

Job declared, "Even though it looks bad, God is actually on my side." That is trust of the highest level seen in the Bible. That is an extraordinary expression of hope.

Job displayed extraordinary courage because he refused to accept defeat. Even though he felt that he could not reach God, he knew God was with him, and he believed that God would rescue him and turn it around in his favor.

That's the lesson that I want to leave with you from this chapter—refuse to accept defeat by the devil. If you live long enough, you will find out that life does not always go the way you want it to go. If you live long enough, you will learn that people do not always act and speak like they should or how you want them to. If you live long enough, you will learn that God cannot be controlled or manipulated. Life brings challenges. Tough, painful, and unexpected challenges. Those challenges will come in all shapes and sizes. They will differ in intensity. They will come at varying intervals. It will not be like Job's trials, but they will come.

We have to make up our minds that God will bring us through because that is what His Word promises. Here is the lesson, refuse to accept defeat by the devil. But that is half of the assignment. What we also have to do is prophesy blessings into our future despite how bad the present may look. Whatever you are going through today, do what Job did and speak blessing into your future.

South-African-born preacher and prophet Kim Clement had a song that our family loved to sing at our family altars. Some of the words were:

> "I'm somewhere in the future... And I look much
> better than I look right now."

In every area of life that may be under attack at the moment, declare victory over it. Speak blessings into your mental and emotional life. Speak blessings into your health, your home, and your family. Declare God's victory into your finances, career, studies, and relationships. Speak blessings from the Word of God over your God-given destiny.

Faith calls us to fight for ourselves and to fight for our future. And part of fighting for our future means prophesying into our future. When I say "prophesy," I mean speak God's Word into the situation.

Job had no one on his side. No one was speaking anything good into his life. Not his best friends or his wife. So Job did it himself. Don't wait for others; go ahead and prophesy God's Word into your future despite how messy the present looks. Prophesy into your future and into your destiny and the destiny of your family. Don't quit on yourself. Don't quit despite how others have treated you. Don't quit despite how unfair life has treated you.

Refuse to accept defeat! You are a threat to the devil because you have a kingdom mantle on you. There is a calling and a divine purpose over your life. You have God's Word within you and a story to share with the world. Stay in the fight for the long haul. Stay in the fight as long as it takes. Don't give up after one prayer. Because who God created you to be is worth fighting for. Don't tell everyone what you are fighting for because people will steal your faith and hope.

Always believe that your best is ahead of you.

The message from Job to the devil was, "Is that the best you got? After all that you did, I am coming through because I have a God."

Joseph refused to accept defeat, and God brought him through being hated, slavery, and imprisonment. David refused to accept defeat as he ran toward Goliath, and God gave him a great victory. Daniel refused to accept defeat, and God protected him in the den of lions. The three Hebrew young men refused to accept defeat although they were threatened with a fiery furnace, and God saved them out of the fire. Esther refused to accept defeat, and God gave her favor with the king, and her enemies were destroyed. Paul and Silas refused to accept defeat despite being beaten and put into the inner prison, and God broke their chains and shackles. Our Savior did not accept defeat as He was nailed to the cross and then laid in the tomb. Glory to God; He rose from the dead and is alive forevermore.

Hit Me with Your Best Shot...It Ain't Over

The message of the whole Bible is that despite the devil doing his best against us, God is on our side; God loves us, and as bad as it looks, God will make this right again.

God did show up for Job with blessings and a breakthrough.

> "After Job had prayed for his friends, the LORD
> restored his fortunes and gave him twice as much as
> he had before."
>
> — Job 42:10 (NIV)

We don't know what we will face in the future. It may be better than 2020/2021. Or it may be worse. But whatever life throws at you, shift your focus to God. Shift your focus from people's opinions to God. Shift your focus from your situation to God. Shift your focus from your emotional and/or mental turmoil to God. Shift your focus from the devil and evil to God.

Despite how it looks now, we can prophesy God's blessings into our future. Somewhere in the future, you will look much better than you look now. Speak the Word of God, and the God of the Word will do the rest.

CHAPTER THREE
Challenge the Chains

We moved to New York City in June 2002. Those early days in Queens were very challenging for us. It was a huge transition for us, as we had moved from Wilmore, Kentucky, with a population of 5,000 people. We struggled financially, lived in a tiny second-floor apartment that often lacked heat, and had one ancient-looking air conditioner in the window that barely worked. We had old hand-me-down furniture, and we did not have a car.

I struggled a lot. I was deeply discouraged and disappointed with my life. I allowed my emotions to rule my life. There were days when I could not believe that was my life. It seemed like happiness moved to a galaxy far, far away and that my hopes and dreams were over. We came up against so many closed doors. Have you ever asked yourself the question, "How did I get here?" Sometimes life may feel like the lyrics from the theme song of the TV show *Friends*, "So no one told you life was gonna be this way…"

I am so grateful to God that He did not let go of me in that deep and dark night of my soul. By the grace of God, we refused to lie down and die. There were days when I would be up till the late hours of the night praying and *fighting* with the Lord. It was there that I developed the habit of walking and praying.

Valerie and I wrote a prayer list on a poster board and hung it up on a wall. Every time a prayer was answered, we would let our daughter, Kimberly, check off the item on the list. Before we moved away from that apartment, the Lord had answered all those prayer requests! Hallelujah! Some of those requests were really big ones, including a Green Card and a car. The first part of our Green Card application took about five weeks to be approved, and even our Jewish lawyer said to us, "You must have prayed really hard!"

We were new immigrants. We did not have the covering of the seminary and its scholarship. We had no credit history. And we lived over 8,000 miles away from our families. We had no close friends near us. We had no safety net. But we learned how to lean on the Lord and how to push through with our prayers and with seasons of fasting. And God came through for us. Amazing miracles were happening in those valley days. We learned that despite the challenges, we did not have to lie down and die. We are the people of God. So many things were against us, but God was for us. We are no ordinary prey. We learned that defeat is not God's will for His people.

> On a Sabbath Jesus was teaching in one of the synagogues, and a woman was there who had been crippled by a spirit for eighteen years. She was bent over and could not straighten up at all. When Jesus saw her, he called her forward and said to her, "Woman, you are set free from your infirmity." (KJV: Woman thou art loosed…) Then he put his hands on her, and immediately she straightened up and praised God. Indignant because Jesus had healed on the Sabbath, the synagogue ruler said to the people, "There are six days for work. So come and be healed on those days, not on the Sabbath." The Lord

answered him, "You hypocrites! Doesn't each of you on the Sabbath untie his ox or donkey from the stall and lead it out to give it water? Then should not this woman, a daughter of Abraham, whom Satan has kept bound for eighteen long years, be set free on the Sabbath day from what bound her?" When he said this, all his opponents were humiliated, but the people were delighted with all the wonderful things he was doing.

— Luke 13:10–17 (NIV)

This is yet another powerful miracle by Jesus. In this incident, a woman bent over for eighteen years is healed. Jesus calls her to Him and declares her liberty and deliverance worth the words, "Woman thou art loosed…" Then Jesus answers a challenge about performing the miracle on the Sabbath.

The Setting

Let's ask some key questions about the setting of this miracle:

Who is this woman?

Jesus describes her as a "daughter of Abraham." So we immediately know that she is an Israelite. She is part of the chosen people of God.

Where is this woman?

We see that she is in the synagogue. She is in the place of worship and prayer. The place for religious instruction. It is the place to connect with God, offer sacrifices to God. It is the place to dedicate one's life to God and to seek God to learn more about God. Can we just say it this way? She is in the right place.

When does Jesus encounter her?

It was the Sabbath. The woman certainly got the day right. It is their holy day. We can safely conclude that she is a religious woman.

What is she doing?

Another fair conclusion is that she is trying to keep the law of Moses. She is a woman who is attempting to please God. And despite her situation, she is still found in the house of God. When we look at these facts of this story, we see a woman in the right place on the right day, doing the right thing. And that is a great setting for a miracle.

Daughter of Abraham

There is something very unique about how Jesus identifies this woman when He calls her a "daughter of Abraham." I cannot recall Jesus doing this very often. Jesus healed many people. We read about lepers, a "woman with an issue of blood," a "widow" whose son had died, a "blind man," a "woman caught in adultery," etc.

But He put this lady into a category. Jesus labels her. Jesus gives her an identity as a daughter of Abraham. She is a part of Israel, the chosen people of God. And if we could shift this miracle to a modern setting, she would be a member of the church. She would be a Christian, a child of God, someone faithful in worship, perhaps a person with a prayer life and good at devotions. She would be someone ready to hear the Word of God and a part of the household of faith. Maybe even serving in the church.

It Is Satan's Work

Then Jesus explained the cause of her problem or illness. She had been bound by Satan. Of course, that was just a stunning revelation because she was someone who was busy in the synagogue on the Sabbath. Those words from Jesus catch us by surprise because she was evidently trying to please God.

The fact that she was bent over and still in the synagogue speaks of faith, testifies of hope. It reinforces her level of commitment. It gives us a glimpse into her pain and desperation. Bent over for eighteen years and still in the synagogue on a Sabbath means this was a faith that has endured and persisted. This reveals a hope that was strong.

Yet this daughter of Abraham was bound by Satan. Jesus did not say demon-possessed, but He revealed to us that she was oppressed in her health. It was Satan who had caused this sickness; it was Satan who was behind the mess in her life, and it was Satan who was in control of this specific area. I believe that people can be saved and yet experience defeat in one or more areas of life. Saved, and yet the devil can rule over an area of life.

The Bible identifies him as "a thief" in John 10:10. The devil comes to steal, kill, and destroy. He goes about like a roaring lion, seeking to destroy, ruin, and hurt people. And that is where I place this daughter of Abraham. Her suffering was the result of the working of the devil. Jesus said Satan had bound her.

Expect Blessings from God

It was a strange request when Jesus called her to Him because she was bent over. That meant that she most likely could not see her surrounding very well. Her view would have been limited, and therefore movement must have been tough. She saw the floor. She obviously would struggle to make eye contact. She may have struggled to hear things. Probably the best times of her day would be when she got to lie down on her bed.

Yet Jesus called her to Him. Jesus obviously did not want to make life harder for her. He did not want to embarrass her even more. He did not wish to hurt her. We know that Jesus could have walked over to her. We know that Jesus could have spoken the word of deliverance from where He was standing like He did with "Lazarus, come forth!" But He must have had a reason to call her to Him.

Here is how I want to explain it. There are many sons and daughters of God who have been bowed down and bent over by life struggles; they have been oppressed or defeated in one or more areas of life. Many Christians have been chained. But they are attributing that to God. They are saying God has given it to them. They are counting it as a blessing and identifying the chains as part of their calling. They see it as their training and shaping.

Yet it is not God's will for them. It is not God's plan or purpose for them. Jesus wants them to come to Him, but they are saying, "Lord, it is Your will for me…" This woman may have gotten to the point of accepting this as part of God's will for her life.

She was so different from some of the others we encountered with Jesus. The woman with the issue of blood spent all her money to get healing. Then she heard about Jesus and said, "If I touch Him, I will be well." Blind Bartimaeus cried out to Jesus for help. When people tried to keep him quiet down, he cried even louder, "Son of David, have mercy on me." The leper asked, "Lord, if You are willing, heal me." Jairus pleaded for his daughter, who was ill and dying, and he took Jesus to his house.

NO ORDINARY PREY

This woman may have settled down in her situation. Maybe she prayed for the first year or the first five years. Then she gave up, calling it God's will. Still in the synagogue after eighteen years meant she had faith in God. Still in the synagogue on the Sabbath after eighteen years tells us that she was not angry with God. Still in the synagogue after eighteen years says that she had accepted the situation as being from God.

Many people do that. They see delay as God's will when they should be bringing it to Jesus. But they are choosing to hold on because it may be from God. But the best way to test it is to pray this way, "Lord, if this is Your will for me, then I accept. I know that You will give me strength to cope. Lord, help me, deliver me, and set me free."

There are things that people are not praying about because they are afraid that they will offend God by questioning His will. Jesus in the garden of Gethsemane prays this prayer just before He was arrested and crucified, "Father, if it is possible, remove this cup from Me… Nevertheless, not My will but Thy will be done…" Jesus dared to ask the Father if there was any way for Him to get out of this suffering ahead of Him. What was Jesus asking? I believe it was to bypass the cross and its suffering. Why did Jesus ask? I don't think that it was because He was being rebellious or because He was fearful. I see it as a pattern for us. "Lord, this is tough on me. Can You remove it? But not my will but Your will be done."

Saint Paul prayed for God to remove the thorn in his flesh. He dared to ask. God said no.

But he asked again; actually, he asked three times. God said no and then told him, "My grace is sufficient for you."

That is my point. Before assuming that this sickness or suffering is God's will for your life, ask Him to give you victory, deliverance, healing, etc. God may say yes, or He may say no. God may say, "Later." But dare to ask.

I challenge you to expect blessings from God and not curses. I challenge you to expect healing, not sickness. I challenge you to expect peace, not trouble; expect joy, not pain or misery. I challenge you to expect victory, not defeat; expect help, not abandonment; expect good things, not bad or evil. Come to the Father in heaven with positive expectations. The Word says, "He who did not spare his own Son, but gave him up for us all—how will he not also, along with him, graciously give us all things?" (Romans 8:32, NIV) His Word overflows with promises for every need in our lives.

God is looking for ways to help people; that is why He gave us the gift and privilege of prayer. God is not looking at a list to find where people are disqualified. Instead, God is looking for gaps or loopholes to bless people.

When the four friends carried the cripple man to Jesus and broke through the roof, Jesus looked at the faith of the friends and healed the man. The cripple may have been disqualified for a miracle, but Jesus saw his friends and said, "Yes, you can have your miracle."

Apostle Paul says that the saved woman sanctifies the unsaved husband. We know that God sends His rain on the just and the unjust. God wants to intervene and help people. Christ Jesus died for us while we were yet sinners. Expect blessings from God. Bring your pain to Jesus. Before you accept that area in which you are bowed down or chained as God's will for your life, why not come to Jesus and check it out?

I suggest an openly honest prayer like,

"Lord, I don't like this… Lord, I hate it… but if it is from You to help me grow, please give me the strength to cope… help me be faithful… but if this is the work of Satan, Lord, break his hold over this area of my life and by the blood of Jesus Christ, set me free. Amen."

There are people labeling their sickness as God's will for their lives. People are calling their broken hearts "God's will." Christians are labeling their messed-up finances as "God's will." Born-again people are calling their unstable emotions "God's will." Even Spirit-filled, tongue-talking people are saying their struggles and pains are "God's will" for them. Some are going so far as to announce that their addictions are God's will for them.

I want to suggest a different approach. Pray this way:

Lord, if this sickness is from You, that's fine with me. But until You tell me personally or send an angel or a prophet to confirm that, I am going to challenge this sickness. Because the will of God that I know is in the Bible, and the Bible says that by Your stripes, I am healed.

Do the same about other challenges you face. Pray that way about your mind and emotional struggles. Pray that way about your home and family problems. Pray that way about your finances. Pray that way concerning any worry, stress, anxiety, fear, or depression. Pray that way against sin, addictions, strongholds, etc. Pray that way in regards to generational sicknesses and curses. Pray that way over your friendships and relationships. Pray about any spiritual dryness.

What is the point? Don't allow Satan to camouflage his chains as God's will!

A Year of Repeats

The woman was bound for eighteen years. We assume that it was not from birth that she was bent over because often, such people were identified as blind from birth, blind from their mother's womb, or crippled since birth. So we can assume that this happened to her at a point in her life.

We can speculate how it happened. But what she had was eighteen years of this painful existence. What kind of life did she have? Can you imagine the loneliness? Can you imagine the pain and suffering? Can you imagine the limitations this sickness placed on her? Maybe her studies were canceled, career cut short, marriage prospects ruined. This woman had eighteen years of sameness. It was eighteen years of pain. It was eighteen years of Satan's oppression. It was eighteen years of being deformed, twisted, and bent over. It was eighteen years of being unable to see people eye to eye with just a limited view of the ground. She had eighteen years of defeat.

If we are not too careful, life can go around in circles. And year in and year out, it will be the same old, same old. That is why we need to challenge the things that oppress us and limit us or hinder us. We need to fight against the things that keep us bent and bowed down.

Concluding Note

Our children freely ask us for things, whether it is big or small, whether they deserve it or not, whether we can afford it or not. They have no sense of restriction or hesitation with what they can come to us. We have a Father in heaven with whom we should have no shame or restriction when we come to Him.

Hebrews 4:16 (NIV) says:

> "Let us then approach God's throne of grace with confidence, so that we may receive mercy and find grace to help us in our time of need."

Jesus said that we need to have faith as a little child. There are things that God may allow in our lives that we may not like. But we understand that it is for our own good. I am not denying that God's will can and often does include suffering. But I am saying, "Challenge the chains because our God is not in the business of making life more difficult. In fact, it is just the opposite. Our God wants to help." I am saying that based on this story, there are too many people labeling things that have them bowed, bent, and chained as God's will when, in fact, it is the work of Satan.

It is not only those outside the church but happening right in the church. Come to the Father with an expectancy that He wants to bless you. Jesus has the power to set us free. He is waiting for us to come unto Him. Jeremiah declared that nothing is too hard for the Lord. My favorite verse in the Bible, Matthew 19:26 (NIV), declares that "...with God all things are possible."

We are no ordinary prey. We should not be passive about the things the devil tries to put on us. We need to fight back against it. Too many powerful people are silent about things that they should be praying against. Too many anointed people are still when they should be binding and casting out the works of the devil. We are no ordinary prey. Let's not label the devil's operations as the will of God. And when we encounter people who are doing that, let's declare their freedom and liberty in the name of Jesus Christ.

CHAPTER FOUR
Protect Your Miracle

God raised my grandfather Timothy Moon from the dead! He was pronounced dead and laid in a morgue. God raised him up. And he went on to become an evangelistic preacher. He went around with his tent preaching the gospel. There were powerful signs and wonders through the ministry God gave to him. Many were saved, miraculously healed, and delivered through his preaching and his prayers.

My grandfather involved his entire family in the ministry. My mom led worship at his meetings. She was probably one of the first women to lead worship during a time when it was unheard of. She even led worship in the Durban City Hall during one of his meetings. My mom and her siblings would help set up and take down the tent, and that included chairs, a stage, sound system, lighting, etc. And they would pass out flyers in the neighborhood where the tent was set up. I remember riding through our town, announcing his meetings through a loud speaker mounted on the roof of his car.

I was too young to fully appreciate what a powerful man of God my grandfather was. And he had an amazing group of friends who regularly prayed and preached with him. Although I missed the opportunity to get to know him better, I believe that because of him, our family has a legacy in the ministry.

Today we have a host of pastors and preachers in our family. My uncle, Pastor Joseph Govender, is one of the best preachers I know and has been my role model. Most of my uncles and aunts continued to actively serve God. An uncle, Bobby Govender, helped build several churches and made many mission trips to Mozambique. As I mentioned elsewhere in the book, my mom practically ran our local church.

Today, we have a fourth-generation family member in ministry, my daughter, Kimberly. Her husband, Sean, is also a pastor. In addition, I have five cousins and their spouses in ministry, plus the parents of three young people who married into our family are pastors, including Kimberly's in-laws. That is not counting my cousins, who are actively involved in their local churches.

God had a powerful mantle on my grandfather and a legacy that he had to pass on. He died, but God was not done with him. *It's not over till it's over* because we are no ordinary prey!

One of the devil's strategies is to cut off people from their calling even before they begin. We see that several times in the Bible with such people as Joseph, Moses, David, and even our Lord and Savior, Jesus Christ.

We are no ordinary prey. Don't let the devil steal your calling or stop you from passing on your mantle to the next generation.

The title of this chapter is self-explanatory. The devil will show up to steal, kill, or destroy the miracle that God gave you. The focus of this book is a reminder that we are no ordinary prey, and we don't have to let the devil get away with anything he tries against the people of God or us. We have to fight back or protect our miracle.

"What can be done for her?" Elisha asked.

Gehazi said, "Well, she has no son and her husband is old."

Then Elisha said, "Call her."

So he called her, and she stood in the doorway.

"About this time next year," Elisha said, "you will hold a son in your arms."

"No, my lord," she objected. "Don't mislead your servant, O man of God!" But the woman became pregnant, and the next year about that same time she gave birth to a son, just as Elisha had told her. The child grew, and one day he went out to his father, who was with the reapers.

"My head! My head!" he said to his father.

His father told a servant, "Carry him to his mother."

After the servant had lifted him up and carried him to his mother, the boy sat on her lap until noon, and then he died.

She went up and laid him on the bed of the man of God, then shut the door and went out. She called her husband and said, "Please send me one of the servants and a donkey so I can go to the man of God quickly and return."

"Why go to him today?" he asked. "It's not the New Moon or the Sabbath."

"It's all right," she said. She saddled the donkey and said to her servant, "Lead on; don't slow down for me unless I tell you." So she set out and came to the man of God at Mount Carmel.

When he saw her in the distance, the man of God said to his servant Gehazi, "Look! There's the Shunammite! Run to meet her and ask her, 'Are you all right? Is your husband all right? Is your child all right?'"

"Everything is all right," she said. When she reached the man of God at the mountain, she took hold of his feet.

Gehazi came over to push her away, but the man of God said, "Leave her alone! She is in bitter distress, but the LORD has hidden it from me and has not told me why."

"Did I ask you for a son, my lord?" she said. "Didn't I tell you, 'Don't raise my hopes'?"

Elisha said to Gehazi, "Tuck your cloak into your belt, take my staff in your hand and run. If you meet anyone, do not greet him, and if anyone greets you, do not answer. Lay my staff on the boy's face."

But the child's mother said, "As surely as the LORD lives and as you live, I will not leave you."

So he got up and followed her.

Gehazi went on ahead and laid the staff on the boy's face, but there was no sound or response. So Gehazi went back to meet Elisha and told him, "The boy has not awakened."

When Elisha reached the house, there was the boy lying dead on his couch. He went in, shut the door on the two of them and prayed to the LORD. Then he got on the bed and lay upon the boy, mouth to mouth, eyes to eyes, hands to hands. As he stretched himself out upon him, the boy's body grew warm. Elisha turned away and walked back and forth in the room and then got on the bed and stretched out upon him once more. The boy sneezed seven times and opened his eyes. Elisha summoned

Gehazi and said, "Call the Shunammite." And he did. When she came, he said, "Take your son."

She came in, fell at his feet and bowed to the ground. Then she took her son and went out.

— 2 Kings 4:14–37 (NIV)

Miracles Under Fire

Satan hates our blessings. He hates our salvation, our health, our family, our marriages, our spiritual lives, our finances, and our progress. He wants to stop that flow of blessings in our lives. John 10:10 reveals His modus operandi—steal, kill, and destroy.

I believe that his goal is to replace genuine blessings with his counterfeit. The rewards of sinful pleasures are momentary. And only after we are trapped do we discover the real consequences of those actions. Let's be honest, the initial stages of an addiction are fun. People get addicted to stuff that is exciting. But sooner rather than later, they discover the chains of addictions, and then it is no longer fun because any addition takes control of one's life.

In the text at the beginning of the chapter, we have a pattern. The miracle becomes a target and is attacked.

> "When an evil spirit comes out of a man, it goes through arid places seeking rest and does not find it. Then it says, 'I will return to the house I left.' When it arrives, it finds the house unoccupied, swept clean and put in order. Then it goes and takes with it seven other spirits more wicked than itself, and they go in

and live there. And the final condition of that man is
worse than the first."

— Matthew 12:43–45 (NIV)

When God delivers a person or a situation and the enemy is
cast out, he tries to get back in. When he finds a gap, he will take
it. We need to make sure that after every breakthrough, we close
the gaps. We can do so with prayer, worship, spending time in the
Word of God, and fellowship with other Christians.

> When the Philistines heard that David had been
> anointed king over Israel, they went up in full force
> to search for him, but David heard about it and went
> down to the stronghold.
>
> — 2 Samuel 5:17 (NIV)

When David was crowned king, the Philistines were even
more motivated to attack him. "Full force" is how the Bible describes their response. When God blesses us, Satan will come out
against us. The greater the blessing, the greater will be his de-
termination to stop us from enjoying the blessings. Miracles do
come under attack.

When Jesus performed miracles, the people questioned those
miracles. The Pharisees and the scribes accused Jesus of having
demonic power. They suggested he was a fake, a scam artist. They
got upset that Jesus performed miracles on the Sabbath, and they
argued it was in violation of God's law. They got upset at the
words Jesus used and His methods.

> Meanwhile a large crowd of Jews found out that
> Jesus was there and came, not only because of him
> but also to see Lazarus, whom he had raised from

the dead. So the chief priests made plans to kill Lazarus as well, for on account of him many of the Jews were going over to Jesus and putting their faith in him.

— John 12:9–11 (NIV)

Wow, their reaction is incredible. Why does the devil attack miracles? There are countless reasons. To show that what God did was fake. To convey the message that prayer does not work, to imply that faith in God is a waste of time. To convince people that God just wanted to play games with them. And to prove that miracles no longer happen. The people who were against Jesus wanted to kill Lazarus to stop others from believing in Him.

We know that miracles boost our faith. Miracles help people get saved and cause revival.

But when the miracle is under fire, or that miracle fades or is lost, then it has the opposite effect. People lose faith and hope; people question the validity of prayer. The people who were inspired by our miracles are affected. They ask, did the person with the testimony lie? I have seen people healed in a service, then walk out and lose their healing. I have seen people revived in church services and lose that fire inside in a week. People do get delivered from addictions, and soon they are back to where they used to be. Then we ask, "Was it real in the first place?" And that is the intention of the enemy.

The Shunammite Woman

The Shunammite woman gets her miracle baby, and then he dies. The father plays a very small role in this story. We hardly hear from him in the first part of the story when the child is born.

When the child is ill, his instruction is to take him to his mother. That is a lesson to be learned by all future fathers—when you do not know what else to do, send them to their mothers!

It is in her actions that we see some powerful lessons on how we can show the devil that we are no ordinary prey when he comes to steal, kill, or destroy the miracles and blessing in our lives. She gets a carriage and makes her way to the man of God; she brings him back, and the boy is raised from the dead. Hallelujah!

Go back to the source of the miracle.

The woman's first action was to get to Elisha. Elisha was the one who prophesied and released the miracle in her life. Whenever you find yourself under pressure in life, remember who your God is and remember who you are. God is the answer. He needs to be the first one that you call upon. He is the reason for all our blessings. When your body hurts, get to your Creator. When your finances are under attack, get to your Provider. When your marriage is in trouble, get to the One who put you together in the first place. When you are broken, get to the Healer. We have to get to the source of life and blessings.

She knew where to find Him.

This woman knew where Elisha was located. Do you know where to find God? Do you know how to get connected to God? It is simple. You will find Him in prayer. You will find Him in worship. You will find Him in actions of faith. You find Him in words of faith. You will find Him in His Word.

She got there in a hurry.

She says to the driver, "Go as fast as you can. Don't let up unless I tell you to. I am a woman, and maybe you think of me as frail or weak or tender or gentle, but this is not the time to slow down on my account. I have a need, and it is urgent." We need the same mentality whenever we feel ourselves under attack from the devil. Get to God quickly. Pray immediately. Don't delay; God is just a prayer away.

She did not tell her husband the full story.

Her husband asks this question, "Why do you have to go now? Because it is not New Moon or Sabbath." This is equivalent to, "Why do you have to go to church today? It is not a Sunday; it isn't Easter or Christmas. Why do you have to pray? Why do you have to fast?" Those are unspiritual comments that come from a worldly perspective. For the husband, God was in a box, so leave Him there. Religion has a box; don't mess with it. Sometimes you cannot tell everyone about the struggles you face; more especially, you do not want to tell someone like her husband. His faith was in a religion compartment. People can dampen your faith. They will criticize your passion. You do not want a person who does not believe in prayer to be praying for your urgent need. You do not want a negative person, a skeptic, or someone who has given up on God to be in charge of your prayer requests. Sometimes we just have to be general about our personal prayer requests.

Positive words.

Notice her first words to the prophet Elisha, "All is well." Those are positive words. What is more, they are prophetic words. A confession that it will be okay. The miracle of having a baby was so awesome. If God did that then, He can do this now. We sing the lyric of the worship song, "The Lord gives and takes away," based on Job's confession. In that story, it was really the devil that took from him. Can I just remind you that God is not vindictive? He does not give blessings only to turn around and take away.

God does take away at times. But not at random, not to mess up lives. God is certainly not out to play head games with people. God is not going to give a marriage and then take it away. God is not going to give healing and then take it away. God is not going to give a deliverance and then take it away. God is not going to give joy and peace and then take it away. He does not operate with pettiness. He is a great, big, awesome God.

We bought bicycles for our children when they were little. But we did not take them away after a few weeks. Even when they were naughty, they had time-out punishments. But what we gave to them, they could keep. We do get to places when we lose blessings because of our rebellion, but I believe that those only happen in extreme cases, and we can get to the point of no return.

> "If you, then, though you are evil, know how to give
> good gifts to your children, how much more will
> your Father in heaven give good gifts to those who
> ask him!"
> — Matthew 7:11 (NIV)

> "For God's gifts and His call are irrevocable."
> — Romans 11:29 (NIV)

He never withdraws them when once they are given, and He does not change His mind about those to whom He gives His grace or to whom He sends His call.

This context concerns God's covenant with the Jews. But there is a lesson that God is not giving with one hand and taking away with another hand. A church that I pastored had many young people who would ask me this question, "What if God wanted me to give up my career, my dreams, my plans?" My response was, "Where are you getting this from? If God asks you to give up a plan, it is only because He has a better plan for your life. God has bigger and better dreams for you than you have for yourself. God is not out to rob people of life and joy. He came to give abundant life." The point is this: when this woman came with a positive confession, she knew that God had given her a gift and miracle in her son.

She knew that God was good. Although there was a setback, she believed that God was good. This stirred up that positive confession. Even under attack, we can still have faith.

And we can still live with hope. God is good, and all the time, He is good. We don't come out with guns blazing against God with attacks of "Why did You do this to me? Why did You allow this?" Instead, "Lord, You blessed me, and that miracle is under attack or has been stolen. I know that You can give it back to me or give me something better."

When the devil took from Job, he still worshipped God. In the end, God gave him double for his trouble. Under pressure, never lose your faith and hope. Because the God who blessed you in the first place is a good God.

Hold on to God.

Elisha sent his servant to pray for her son, but she held on to Him. It is good that others pray for us, and I encourage you to share prayer requests. I believe in intercessions. Others' prayers on our behalf make a difference. We believe that others' faith can bless us. But beyond what others can do, fight for your miracle. You hold on to God yourself. It is not enough that others are praying for you; get with God yourself. Be desperate before God yourself. The best person to express to God what you are feeling and how you are hurting is yourself.

Application

Satan loves to steal, kill, and destroy what God gives and does in our lives. So expect his attacks. But more than that, understand the purpose behind them. He wants to undermine what God did to hinder your faith and to discourage the faith of others around you.

Stay grateful to God. Continually pray over what God has done in your life. And stay alert for any "gaps" that the enemy is trying to open up in your lives, specifically in the areas where you have gained a miracle or a victory.

Most of all, do not let the devil get away with anything. Let's take back what the enemy stole from us. Take back your good health and strength in Jesus' name. Take back your peace of mind. Take back your joy. Take back your family unity. Take back your dreams and plans. Take back your finances. Take back the destiny that he may have detoured or distracted.

Miracles come under attack, so keep praying for the covering and protection of the blood of Jesus over your lives, homes, marriages, finances, jobs, studies, relationships, and your destiny.

I believe that we are entering a season of restoration, recovery, renewal, revival, and resurrection!

CHAPTER FIVE
Silencing the Giants

I am grateful to God for the teaching that revealed that our minds are the battlefield. When I was in my early twenties, I was harshly treated by people who really should have provided a covering for me. The people who should have prayed with me and mentored me pushed me aside. It hurt me deeply. And it also consumed my thoughts. Those people would be on my mind even before I washed my face in the morning. Angry and bitter thoughts consumed me throughout the day and were with me when I got to bed at night. I was tormented. I prayed the blood of Jesus Christ against those thoughts. I kept praying that over and over and over again. And yet those thoughts persisted. I played worship music. And yet those tormenting thoughts stayed with me. I got into the Word of God. And I still struggled.

Those thoughts persisted, but I also persisted in praying, worshipping, and the Word. And one day, I awoke and realized that those tormenting thoughts were gone. I was not sure exactly when it happened. But God delivered me. Hallelujah! Because prayer works. Because worship makes a difference. There is such power in anointed songs and music. Because something happens within us when we get into the Word of God. Because there is power in the blood of Jesus.

This is how you know you have the victory over something painful; it is when you think about it, and it does not hurt you. This is how you know you have the victory over anger and bitterness; it is when the names of the people who betrayed you come up in conversation, and it does not unsettle you. This is how you know that you have victory over any offense; it is when you can pray blessings over those who set out to harm you.

The devil wants to keep us off balance and in a deep, dark place because of the hurts in our life. If we let him, the devil will rule over our thoughts and emotions. But we have to be committed to pressing on to the victory that we know is possible in our Savior, Christ Jesus.

> "Now the Philistines gathered their forces for war…Saul and the Israelites assembled and camped…and drew up their battle line to meet the Philistines. The Philistines occupied one hill and the Israelites another, with the valley between them."
> — 1 Samuel 17:1–3 (NIV)

The time of the Judges was a rough period in Israel's history. The Philistines were their archenemies. The Philistines had the upper hand a lot of the time. This chapter records another one of the battles between the two nations.

> A champion named Goliath, who was from Gath, came out of the Philistine camp. His height was six cubits and a span. He had a bronze helmet on his head and wore a coat of scale armor of bronze weighing five thousand shekels; on his legs he wore bronze greaves, and a bronze javelin was slung on his back. His spear shaft was like a weaver's rod, and its

iron point weighed six hundred shekels. His shield
bearer went ahead of him.

— 1 Samuel 17:4–7 (NIV)

We meet the antagonist, Goliath. There are various interpretations of his height. Some put him at nine feet, while others say eleven feet tall. The bottom line is he was tall and massive. The description of his armor tells us that he was big and tall and strong. In the Bible, we do read about a race of giants called the Nephilim (Genesis 6) and Rephaites (Deuteronomy 2). And there are accounts of David and his men battling giants.

Goliath is the most famous of all giants in the Bible. He had brothers and family members who were giants too. And we learn that their origins were evil. And they almost always were representative of evil in the Bible.

Goliath stood and shouted to the ranks of Israel,
"Why do you come out and line up for battle? Am
I not a Philistine, and are you not the servants of
Saul? Choose a man and have him come down to
me. If he is able to fight and kill me, we will become
your subjects; but if I overcome him and kill him,
you will become our subjects and serve us." Then the
Philistine said, "This day I defy the armies of Israel!
Give me a man and let us fight each other."

— 1 Samuel 17:8–10 (NIV)

Goliath offered a challenge to the Israelites to fight a one-to-one battle, which was a nice-sounding plan. Why let everyone risk death when only one can die for the nation? Of course, it was a good plan for him because he was the biggest and strongest.

There really was no contest. It was a slam dunk in his favor. The Hebrew word for "defy" is *charaph*. That means "to scorn, mock or regard as having little worth."

> "On hearing the Philistine's words, Saul and all the
> Israelites were dismayed and terrified."
> — 1 Samuel 17:11 (NIV)

The Hebrew word for Israel's reaction is *chathath*. That means "to be broken down with fear or broken in pieces." The second word is *yare'*, and that means "terrified and filled with dread."

> "Whenever the Israelites saw the man, they all fled
> from him in great fear."
> — 1 Samuel 17:24 (NIV)

This verse reveals more of their reaction. Goliath's words terrified them, and they ran and hid. The very sight of him put them to flight.

> "For forty days the Philistine came forward every
> morning and evening and took his stand."
> — 1 Samuel 17:16 (NIV)

Intimidation

Goliath intimidated Israel. "Intimidation" means "a threat, pressure, bullying, or terrorizing." Giants are larger than life. They are symbolic of things that are bigger than what we can handle. Giants in life are representative of things that are intimidating.

Let's look at some responses to intimidation:

Fear

Israel was terrified by Goliath and his words. Intimidation causes fear, dread, and panic. It will terrorize people. Have you ever used the words "I am scared to death"?

Hinders

Intimidation stops us from our usual, normal activities. Israel did not go to battle; instead, they ran and hid. Intimidation stops us from going about with daily activities.

Silences

Israel was so terrified that they could not answer Goliath. There is a level of intimidation that will shut you up. It will silence your prayers and your praise.

Controls

Closely connected to hindering is controlling. Goliath's war cry set the pattern for Israel's day. He was large and in charge. Have you ever been intimated just by someone showing up? Maybe it unsettled you and made you fearful and worried or set you in panic mode. We are not free to be ourselves. We cannot say or do what we would like to. When we cannot be ourselves, that means we are living with intimidation.

Anti-Christ

Anything that stops us from being who God created us to be and works against God's purpose for us, that thing is demonic. It is against God. It is the spirit of the Anti-Christ.

AM and PM

"For forty days the Philistine came forward every morning and evening and took his stand."

— 1 Samuel 17:16 (NIV)

Morning and evening are key elements in this story. I want to tell you this is a demonic strategy. What they heard in the morning from Goliath affected their entire day. At the start of their day, Israel was terrified, and at the close of the day, Israel was terrified. Goliath's threats framed their day. His words opened and closed their day.

That was a clever and cunning strategy, the AM and PM threats. At the start of their day, Israel was already in fear. At the start of their day, Israel was on the run. Often the things that happen early in the morning can ruin the entire day. We use the expression "I got off on the wrong side of the bed." Israel must have spent the rest of the day wondering when the next threat would come.

What they heard in the evening affected their sleep and their dreams. They most likely could not rest at night. Think about this for a moment. When we hear something that upsets us, we have no rest, no peace, and we cannot think straight.

You will live in constant suspense, filled with dread both night and day, never sure of your life. In the morning you will say, "If only it were evening!" and in the evening, "If only it were morning!"—because of the terror that will fill your hearts and the sights that your eyes will see.

— Deuteronomy 28:66–67 (NIV)

God gave this warning if the people of Israel rebelled. And this is what happened to them.

What is framing your day? What is speaking to you at the start of your day? What is talking to you at the close of your day? Goliath's words opened and closed their day.

Giant Speak

Maybe I should ask this question this way—what "giants" are speaking to you? What did Goliath use to intimidate Israel? He used "his threats." In other words, his words. Are you tuned into "giant-speak"? What "giant-speak" is robbing you of your joy and stealing your peace? What "giant-speak" is keeping you up at night?

There are also the inaudible threats of giants. In other words, negative thoughts. Thoughts may not be audible, but they certainly have a voice inside our minds. Vain imagination is another issue. Sometimes negative thoughts run wild in our minds. The Bible talks about vain imaginations. Our minds can go a million miles a minute. One small word or thought can send our minds to ungodly conclusions. Negative thoughts can harass us. Fears and insecurities also speak to us. Bad experiences tend to always have access to the "replay" button in our minds.

The devil uses words against us. Negative words that we heard. Ugly words, critical words, curses, unkind words, hate-filled words, etc. The problem with the words, whether audible or in our thoughts, is that they can intimidate us, silence us, control us and hold us back from God's purposes. Words are the weapons in the battlefield of the mind.

Identify the "giant-speak" intimidating you. The devil knows how to keep us off balance. He knows how to steal our peace. He knows what buttons to push and how to rock our world.

David's Discernment

David showed up, and the battle changed. Let's look at what David did.

> David asked the men standing near him, "What will be done for the man who kills this Philistine and removes this disgrace from Israel? Who is this uncircumcised Philistine that he should defy the armies of the living God?"
> — First Samuel 17:26 (NIV)

Who is he?

David put a label on him and called him "uncircumcised." That had nothing to do with the physical, but it meant that Goliath was outside the covenant with God. He had no relationship with God. If he had no relationship with God, then he was operating with a demonic agenda.

David implies, "How dare his words intimidate us? How dare his words limit us and control us?" In other words, why should the devil's words control us? Put a label on the threats. Call it what it is—demonic, satanic, evil, and wicked. We have to recognize the origin of the things that threaten us and intimidate us.

If you can name it, identify it, it will be easier to face it. It will be easier to confront it and deal with it.

Who are we?

David did not stop at labeling Goliath; he said, "We are the army of God, the Living God." I don't even have to expand on that line; it is self-explanatory. When we know who we are and who we belong to, it will change how we feel about ourselves and how we feel about life. When we know who we are and who we belong to, it will change how we look at the challenges, setbacks, and attacks against us. And it will change how we decide to move forward. When we know who we are and who we belong to, it will encourage us, empower us, and enable us to take a stand. So who are you? Who do you belong to?

What is going on?

David says something powerful in that verse, "This is a disgrace on Israel." The Hebrew word is *cherpah*. David was reminding them that the words of this giant had brought shame and disgrace on them. It was embarrassing. It was humiliating. It dishonored and degraded who they were and who they belonged to. I believe that David was saying, "This is not who we are; we are better than this!"

Don't accept the threats of the devil as part of life. It is not who we are. It is not our destiny. It is not the way God wants us to live. We need discernment as to whether it is God or the devil. We need to ask what the origin of these attacks against us is. Discernment helps us put the correct labels on things. Instead of blaming God, we can rise up and cancel the enemy's words.

David's Prophetic Actions

> David said to Saul, "Let no one lose heart on ac-
> count of this Philistine; your servant will go and
> fight him."
>
> — 1 Samuel 17:32 (NIV)

David did more than just put labels. David did more than just
correctly identify what was going on. David did more than exercise discernment. David did something about it when he went to
war against the giant. Just knowing is not enough; we have to do
something about it. We have experts who know everything about
everything. And they are good at telling what is wrong.

> He said to David, "Am I a dog, that you come at me
> with sticks?" And the Philistine cursed David by his
> gods. "Come here," he said, "and I'll give your flesh
> to the birds and the wild animals!"
>
> — 1 Samuel 17:43–44 (NIV)

Goliath, seeing David, threatened him and cursed him. The
entire army fled in terror when Goliath spoke. But David had
another response.

> David said to the Philistine, "…I come against you
> in the name of the LORD Almighty, the God of the
> armies of Israel… This day the LORD will deliver you
> into my hands, and I'll strike you down and cut
> off your head… All those gathered here will know
> that… the battle is the LORD's, and he will give all of
> you into our hands."
>
> — 1 Samuel 17:45–47 (NIV)

David did not respond to his words; instead, David declared the power of God's name. David was saying, "Your threats are meaningless against God's name." That is what we have to do against the devil, declare victory in the name of Jesus. Every knee must bow to that holy name of Jesus. Jesus is the name that is above all names! Don't take the devil's bait; instead, proclaim Jesus' name!

David prophesied victory; he said, "I am going to kill you, cut off your head, and then kill the rest of your crew." David declared, "The battle belongs to the Lord, and God is going to give me the victory." David did cut off his head and silenced him once and for all. That is the way to silence the giants. Pray against the thoughts that intimidate us in the name of Jesus Christ and believe that God will set you free.

Start your day off by prophesying into your day, "Today is the day that the Lord has made; I will rejoice and be glad in it. Today, God's grace is sufficient and enough for every challenge I face. Today, God will fight my battles. Today, no weapon formed against me will prosper. Today, I am healed and spirit-filled. Today, I am led by the Spirit. Today, I am the head and not the tail. Today, I am loaded with blessings."

When you go to bed at night, remind yourself of Psalm 121, that God never slumbers nor sleeps, and that He will protect you by day and by night. Open and close your day with the Word of God.

> David left Zadok the priest and his fellow priests before the tabernacle of the LORD… to present burnt offerings to the LORD on the altar of burnt offering

regularly, morning and evening, in accordance with everything written in the Law of the LORD...

> — 1 Chronicles 16:39–40 (NIV)

Why did God institute a morning and evening sacrifice? So that they would open and close the day in worship. So that they would acknowledge God and His hand over them at the start of the day and at the close of the day. Israel went through their day knowing God loved them and went to bed at night knowing that He loved them. There was a morning and evening reminder of how God saved them. There was a morning and evening reminder that there was a calling on them as a nation. There was a morning and evening reminder that they were special to Him. There was a morning and evening reminder that God had a purpose for them in the world.

> They were also to stand every morning to thank and praise the LORD. They were to do the same in the evening.
>
> — 1 Chronicles 23:30 (NIV)

Israel expressed their gratefulness to God in the morning and in the evening. Praise God at the start of your day and at the end of the day.

> "As for me, I call to God, and the LORD saves me. Evening, morning and noon I cry out in distress, and he hears my voice. He rescues me unharmed from the battle waged against me, even though many oppose me."
>
> — Psalm 55:16–18 (NIV)

David framed his day with prayer and praise in the morning and evening, and he praised God in the middle of the day too.

> Keep this Book of the Law always on your lips; meditate on it day and night, so that you may be careful to do everything written in it. Then you will be prosperous and successful. Have I not commanded you? Be strong and courageous. Do not be afraid; do not be discouraged, for the LORD your God will be with you wherever you go.
> — Joshua 1:8–9 (NIV)

Joshua had stepped into leadership, and he was about to lead his people into the promised land. God gave him this instruction, "Focus on My Word in the morning and in the evening." Joshua started his day with God's promises and closed his day with them.

Goliath's Location

One more quick lesson from this story. Goliath threatened, and everyone ran and hid. He did this for forty days, both morning and evening. Why did it not occur to him to come off the mountain and rush at the Israelite army? It is my opinion that if he had done that, they would have run and not stopped running, probably until they got to the English Channel.

So here's the biggest question, why did he stay in the same place? If his voice and appearance terrorized them from a distance, why not get near them? It makes no sense that he stayed in place for forty days. Did he lack confidence? Was he afraid? Was he too lazy to take a few steps?

We know that everything in the Bible is significant. We know that there are lessons in the names of people and places, in the sequence of events, and in the time of day. So there was something significant about Goliath's location.

"They pitched camp at Ephes Dammim…"
— 1 Samuel 17:1 (NIV)

The Hebrew meaning of *Ephes Dammim* is "edge of blood or boundary of blood drops." *Some of you know what I am about to say…* The enemy of God's people could not cross the bloodline!

The devil's threats may have shaken you. His threats may upset you, frighten you. The devil's words may have hindered your day and frustrated your nights. But he can't touch you. They're just words because he cannot cross the bloodline of Jesus that is around you. And the blood of Jesus covers you on the left and the right, in the front and in back, above and below, inside and outside. Don't let the threats of the devil rattle you because greater is your God!

I love this Chris Tomlin song:

> *Our God is greater, our God is stronger*
> *God You are higher than any other*
> *Our God is Healer, awesome in power*
> *Our God, Our God*
> *And if Our God is for us, then who could ever stop us*
> *And if our God is with us, then what can stand against?*

Goliath could not cross over because there was something holding Him back in place until David arrived. Today the devil cannot touch you because God is protecting you. The devil is a roaring lion. Have you noticed that when a lion goes on the prowl, it is silent before it pounces on its prey? The devil is just making noise, but he cannot touch you. God has a hedge around you. Don't let his words live in your mind. Develop a morning and evening routine to fill your mind and heart with God's Word.

A Season

One more lesson. Goliath threatened Israel for forty days. Forty in the Bible is symbolic of a season. Israel was forty years in the wilderness; Moses was forty days on the mountain; Elijah went on a forty-day fast, and Jesus spent forty days in the wilderness.

Israel became conditioned to respond to Goliath in fear and terror. It became their pattern. David showed up, and the season ended! *I prophetically declare* that the season of intimidation by your giants is over!

Concluding Note

Step up to battle the devil because you are a child of God. Silence the giants by connecting with God. Pray and declare His Word. Open and close your day with prayer and praise. It will set in motion your victory over satanic intimidation. It will break any mind control that he has over us. Don't let the devil rule your day or mess up your nights. Expel the enemy. You are holy ground. Remember that God is greater, and He has His hedge around you. There is a supernatural border and boundary over you.

CHAPTER SIX
Preach to Yourself

I am a pastor who loves to share the ministry. I am not the kind of pastor who has to preach every sermon, sing every song, pray every prayer, etc. The reason that I am that way is that Valerie and I grew up in the Full Gospel Church of God in South Africa, where ministry was teamwork. I learned to do ministry because my pastors gave me the opportunity to lead worship, preach, teach, and take leadership over cell groups. A lot of what I learned about ministry happened in my home and in the context of my local church (Hermon Temple, Verulam, South Africa). My first pastor was in charge of seven churches, so he was only able to come to our assembly one Sunday in the month. For the rest of the time, my mom fulfilled that role of leading the church. It was unofficial because no women were even allowed to serve on the church council or even preach on a Sunday. My mom did everything except lead the men's ministry!

My training in ministry preceded my going to Bible College. My uncle, Pastor Joseph Govender, who also served as my pastor for many years and has been the spiritual head of our family circle, has been a great inspiration and role model to me.

I said all of that to say this, Valerie and I understand the importance of ministry partners. I am grateful to God for the many anointed people that He gave to us. I thank God for the encouragers, the prayer partners, and the helpers that stood with us. Many have been like Aaron and Hur to us (see Exodus 17). We have been blessed by prophetic people who declared God's word over our lives. We know that ministry is teamwork.

Many pastors will testify of what I am about to say—ministry is also a very lonely place. We had best friends and prayer partners turn against us for no apparent reason. We have had some heart-breaking moments as ministry partners became "active" enemies against us. People that we loved and shared the ministry with did not just pull away from us but tried to discredit and destroy us. Obviously, those actions and words hurt us.

If it were not for the Holy Spirit, we would not have survived those moments. It was the Holy Spirit that reminded us of who we are in God. If we believed every negative word that was said against us, we would have lost our focus on our calling and our purpose. If we allowed the betrayal to determine our value in God, the devil would have walked all over us. The Bible says that Holy Spirit is our Comforter. And He is the One who brings into remembrance the Word of God in us. John 14:26 (NIV) says, "But the Advocate, the Holy Spirit, whom the Father will send in my name, will teach you all things and will remind you of everything I have said to you."

There may be times in life when you are all alone. You may be abandoned, deserted, and betrayed by people you loved and trusted. It is in those moments that we need the help of the Holy Spirit to rise up. There is a powerful lesson in the life of David that perfectly illustrates this lesson.

David

Perhaps the best example of a person of joy in the Bible is the psalmist David. He knew how to sing and dance and how to celebrate God. David knew what true joy was all about. So many psalms that he wrote overflow with the message of joy. But David also knew what it meant to be in trouble. And we can learn a lesson from him about joy.

> David and his men reached Ziklag on the third day. Now the Amalekites had raided the Negev and Ziklag. They had attacked Ziklag and burned it, and had taken captive the women and all who were in it, both young and old. They killed none of them, but carried them off as they went on their way. When David and his men came to Ziklag, they found it destroyed by fire and their wives and sons and daughters taken captive. So David and his men wept aloud until they had no strength left to weep. David's two wives had been captured—Ahinoam of Jezreel and Abigail, the widow of Nabal of Carmel. David was greatly distressed because the men were talking of stoning him; each one was bitter in spirit because of his sons and daughters but David encouraged himself in the LORD his God.
>
> — 1 Samuel 30:1–6 (NIV)

This incident happened during the time that David was on the run from King Saul. In this text, David and his men had gone off to battle, and when they returned, all their stuff had been taken, including their wives and children. It goes without saying that they were upset. But then it got to a tipping point when the deep hurt turned into anger. Angry people often look for someone to blame. Obviously, the men blamed David. They spoke about stoning him. I have to point out that they had nothing when they joined David. It was under David's leadership that they evolved into a mighty army. It was because of David's walk with God that they were blessed. But at this point, they blame David. And they wanted to kill David.

David was all alone. He had lost too. He was also hurting. The Bible says that David was greatly distressed. The Hebrew word is *yatsar*. It means "to be in a narrow strait, to be cramped, besieged, or boxed in." It is a wonderful description of David's anguish. Have you ever been so hurt that you felt that you could not even breathe? That is how David was feeling.

What did the sweet psalmist of Israel do? His response to the pain and sorrow and trouble is powerful. David encouraged himself in the Lord. The Hebrew word is *chazaq*. The word means "to grow strong, to be revived, to restore strength." It also means "to make bold, to become courageous." The word means "to tie or fasten, to hold or grip onto something tightly."

David was in trouble. He was under pressure emotionally. He was in serious physical danger. Then he took a hold of God. It reminds me of Jacob in Genesis 32, who took a hold of God and said to the Lord, "I will not let You go until You bless me." David encouraged himself in God.

And when he did that, the joy started to flow in. He found a safe place. He tapped into supernatural peace and rest. His strength was being renewed and restored. Wisdom started to flow into him. He was able to rise up and motivate his men. The same men who wanted to kill him, he led them in battle. They had a mighty victory, and they got back everything that the enemy had taken from them.

Application

David was alone. He did not have the prophet Samuel with him; by this time, Samuel had died. He did not have prophets with him because he was in exile. David was alone. He did not have the tabernacle with him. He did not have priests to consult. He did not have the ark of the covenant with him. David was alone. He had nobody to tell him it was going to be okay. He had no one to hold his hand. He had no one to hug him or put their arms around his shoulder. David was alone.

So who helped him? He helped himself. Who motivated him? He motivated himself. Who encouraged him? He encouraged himself. How did he do that? I want to suggest that he started to speak to himself. And here is what I think he may have said to himself.

> But you, Lord, are a shield around me, my glory, the One who lifts my head high.
>
> — Psalm 3:3 (NIV)

> Fill my heart with joy when their grain and new wine abound. In peace I will lie down and sleep, for you alone, Lord, make me dwell in safety.
>
> — Psalm 4:7–8 (NIV)

> For surely, O LORD, you bless the righteous; you surround them with your favor as with a shield.
>
> — Psalm 5:12 (NIV)

> The LORD has heard my cry for mercy; the LORD accepts my prayer. All my enemies will be ashamed

and dismayed; they will turn back in sudden
disgrace.

— Psalm 6:9–10 (NIV)

O LORD my God, I take refuge in you; save and
deliver me from all who pursue me.

— Psalm 7:1 (NIV)

The LORD is a refuge for the oppressed, a stronghold in times of trouble. Those who know your
name will trust in you, for you, LORD, have never
forsaken those who seek you.

— Psalm 9:9–10 (NIV)

The Lord is my Shepherd… Yea though I walk
through the valley of the shadow of death—I will
fear no evil… He prepares a table for me in the
presence of my enemies.

— Psalm 23:1, 4–5 (NIV)

The LORD is my light and my salvation—whom
shall I fear? The LORD is the stronghold of my
life—of whom shall I be afraid? When evil men
advance against me to devour my flesh, when my
enemies and my foes attack me, they will stumble
and fall. Though an army besiege me, my heart will
not fear; though war break out against me, even then
will I be confident.

— Psalm 27:1–3 (NIV)

"Your servant has killed both the lion and the bear…
The LORD who delivered me from the paw of the

lion and the paw of the bear will deliver me from the hand of this Philistine."

— 1 Samuel 17:36–37 (NIV)

I believe that David started to rehearse in his mind what God did for him in the past. David started to recall who God was to him and who he was to God. How do you encourage yourself in God? Firstly, you have to know God to encourage yourself in God. And how do you know God? You discover Him in His Word. When we talk about encouraging ourselves, that comes from the Word of God. When you are under stress and pressure, draw encouragement from the Bible. When you are afraid or worried or being bombarded by fearful words, draw your strength from the Word of the Lord.

Everyone needs pastors who can preach to them. Everyone needs Bible teachers to teach them the Word of God. But those pastors and teachers cannot be with you twenty-four seven. That is when you need to be your own preacher. Learn how to preach to yourself. Learn how to prophesy to yourself. When the devil is preaching to you, and when angry people are preaching to you, when people who hate you are preaching to you, when negative words are sent to you, you need to rise up and preach to yourself.

We already know that Satan often attacks when you are alone. The Word of God is powerful. It is a weapon in the spiritual realm. It is called the sword of the Spirit. When we speak the Word of God, it changes the atmosphere. When we speak the Word of God, spiritual warfare takes place, and demons will flee, and the angels will come to minister to us. When we speak the Word of God, the heavens open, and God's glory will fill the place. When we speak the Word of God, changes happen within us. When we speak the Word of God, our souls are fed; our emotions are refreshed. When we speak the Word of God, our faith is ignited, and our hope is boosted.

We know that faith comes by hearing the Word of God. When the Word of God works in us, it will start to work through us. And it will affect the people around us. They will notice something different about us. When we speak the Word of God, it impacts situations.

Preach to yourself whatever your need may be. Find a Bible verse or story that applies to your specific battle. Then preach it to yourself. For example, "In the Bible, God healed the lame, the sick, and the blind; God can heal me too!" Preach to yourself, "By His stripes, I am healed." Preach to yourself, "My God shall supply all my needs." Preach to yourself, "I am more than a conqueror." Preach to yourself, "God's angels surround me and protect me." Preach to yourself, "The blood of Jesus cleanses me from all my sin, and I am a new creation in Christ Jesus."

You don't need a correct reference in terms of chapter and verse. You just need to believe that the Word of God is true. Spend time in the Word of God. Become your own best preacher. When you feel down, preach to yourself. When you feel discouraged, preach to yourself. When you feel overwhelmed, preach to yourself. When you feel like you are losing your peace, losing your mind, losing your hope, preach to yourself. When you feel like you are losing the fight, preach to yourself. When you feel all alone and isolated, preach to yourself.

Ephesians 6 says the Word of God is the sword of the Spirit. If St. Paul was writing today, he might say the Word of God is the AK-47 of the Spirit. It is a weapon. But a weapon without bullets has a limited ability to protect you. You need bullets. You need Bible verses committed to memory, so when you are under attack, you can quote them to yourself.

Daniel

While he was saying this to me, I bowed with my
face toward the ground and was speechless. Then
one who looked like a man touched my lips, and I
opened my mouth and began to speak. I said to the
one standing before me, "I am overcome with anguish because of the vision, my lord, and I feel very
weak. How can I, your servant, talk with you, my
lord? My strength is gone and I can hardly breathe."
Again the one who looked like a man touched me
and gave me strength. "Do not be afraid, you who
are highly esteemed," he said. "Peace! Be strong now;
be strong."

— Daniel 10:15–19 (NIV)

The angel comes with a message. Daniel is overwhelmed by the
vision and is knocked out. Then the angel speaks to him, and
Daniel says, "When he spoke to me, I was strengthened." It is
the same Hebrew word—*chazaq*. Look at some of the words the
angel uses, "greatly beloved," "fear not," "peace," and "be strong."
When you have no one to speak to you, preach to yourself. Find
Bible verses that tell you that God loves you and that God is interested in your situation.

Don't preach nonsense to yourself. Stop saying, "God hates
me," "No one loves me," or "I am such an idiot." Then you are just
agreeing with the devil. Preach the Word of God. Stop agreeing
with the devil and start agreeing with the Word of God.

CHAPTER SEVEN
Prophetic Praise

Valerie and I grew up in families that had family altars. A family altar is what we call our family prayer time. Valerie's parents would gather their family together on a Wednesday evening for their time of prayer. My family prayed together almost every day. So naturally, when we had our own family, praying together every day was an important part of our lives. Our family altar included testifying of the blessings of that day, reading a Bible text, and prayer. We often anointed each other with oil and even shared Holy Communion regularly.

Praising God was also an important part of our family altar. Most days, we would play a CD with praise music and dance before the Lord. Kimberly, Jordan, and I loved those times when we danced extravagantly before the Lord. There were times when we would write down our prayer requests and pray over them. Sometimes we would place them on the floor and circle them as we prayed. But at other times, we would dance around them and declare victory even before we got the answer.

We have been called to praise God. It is important to praise God for what He does in our lives. And it is equally important to praise God even before you get the answer.

One of the most well-loved chapters in the Bible is 2 Chronicles 20. It tells of the time that King Jehoshaphat and Judah were attacked by a vast army comprising of three nations. Those enemy nations were bigger and stronger than Judah.

The people of God came before the Lord in prayer and fasting to ask for His help. That is the best response when you are in trouble: call on the Lord. Jehoshaphat called for a fast. Fasting is a turbocharged prayer. Fasting takes us to a higher level of spiritual warfare.

> He said: "Listen, King Jehoshaphat and all who live
> in Judah and Jerusalem! This is what the LORD says
> to you: 'Do not be afraid or discouraged because
> of this vast army. For the battle is not yours, but
> God's.'"
>
> — 2 Chronicles 20:15 (NIV)

The Lord gave them a prophetic word that the battle belonged to Him. The man who spoke that word was Jahaziel. He was a Levite, which meant that he was a priest. But he was also a descendent of Asaph, who was appointed by David as the chief singer. This priest was a worshipper!

One of the best ways to hear the voice of God is to be a worshipper. Worship changes the atmosphere. Worship makes us more sensitive to the voice of God. Worship prepares us to receive from God.

The man of God told them to show up at the battlefield and take their positions and watch God do the rest.

> "Then some Levites from the Kohathites and Kora-
> hites stood up and praised the LORD, the God of
> Israel, with a very loud voice."
>
> — 2 Chronicles 20:19 (NIV)

The response of the people to the word from God was to praise God. We need to get excited anytime we hear a word from God. God's word is truth.

> As they began to sing and praise, the LORD set ambushes against the men of Ammon and Moab and Mount Seir who were invading Judah, and they were defeated. The Ammonites and Moabites rose up against the men from Mount Seir to destroy and annihilate them. After they finished slaughtering the men from Seir, they helped to destroy one another.
> — 2 Chronicles 20:22–23 (NIV)

As the people of Judah started to sing and worship God, the enemy nations turned on each other. They killed each other. The Ammonites and Moabites joined forces against the men of Seir, and then they turned on each other.

> When the men of Judah came to the place that overlooks the desert and looked toward the vast army, they saw only dead bodies lying on the ground; no one had escaped. So Jehoshaphat and his men went to carry off their plunder, and they found among them a great amount of equipment and clothing and also articles of value—more than they could take away. There was so much plunder that it took three days to collect it.
> — 2 Chronicles 20:24–25 (NIV)

The people of God walked in only to find dead bodies. Not a single person had escaped. They took three days to collect the plunder. And on day four, they had a praise and worship service.

The fear of God came on all the nations, and God gave them peace.

Application #1—Prophetic Praise Explained

God gave this promise, "I will fight your battle." Then God said, "Stand still and see what I will do." This is important—there was no instruction for Jehoshaphat to praise and worship God. He did this on his own initiative. God did not say, "Sing, play music, or dance for My glory." There was no directive saying, "Get the praise team ahead of the army." It was King Jehoshaphat, led by the Spirit of God, that came up with this plan.

He got a word, a promise from God. And on the authority and power of that word, the king said, "Let's praise God." With a belief and strong confidence in the Word, the king said, "Let's sing." He was so badly outnumbered, but he had a word from God. So he said, "Let's dance before the Lord." He was outgunned, but he had a word from God. So he said, "Let's worship."

There is no evidence that anything was happening in their favor. All he had was a word from God, and that was good enough for him to glorify God. Nothing had changed. The word of God was all he needed to put his praise boots on! He had the initiative to praise God. He did not wait till after the battle. He did not hold off until they had the victory. Jehoshaphat and the people praised God ahead of the miracle. He did not wait until the battle started or the middle of the battle; he got his praise boots on from the get-go!

That is the opposite of what most people do. We wait to praise after the thing is done. We testify when it is complete. What Jehoshaphat was doing is what we call prophetic praise. Prophetic in this sense that it had to do with the future. He was praising God for something that God had yet to do.

The whole idea of the prophetic is speaking the word of God that may not necessarily match the reality or the facts. A prophet speaks things that are yet to be and what God is going to do. It is mostly concerned with the future. Often, a prophetic word will be the opposite of what we may be seeing, hearing, feeling, tasting, or experiencing.

Prophetic praise is saying, "I cannot see it, but thank You, Lord, for the Word, which says it is possible." Prophetic praise is declaring, "I cannot hear it, but thank You, Lord, for the Word, which says it is possible." Prophetic praise announces, "I cannot smell or taste or touch it, but thank You, Lord, for the Word, which says it is possible." Prophetic praise is going by faith in the Word. Isn't that what Christianity is all about? It is faith in the unseen.

Jehoshaphat praised for something that had not yet happened. Do you want to take a moment to pause reading and praise God for something you are waiting for?

Application #2—Prophetic Praise Is Warfare

When they praised and worshipped God, He gave them the victory He promised. Praise is warfare. When we praise God, the devil and his demons are confused. When we praise God, demonic alliances will turn on themselves. *Hallelujah! Thank You, Jesus!*

When we praise God, He shows up with His power. When we praise God, He moves on our behalf. When we praise God, we will get the victory. Praise is warfare.

Like Jehoshaphat, if you find yourself in a situation that makes you feel overwhelmed, praise God. If ever you feel outnumbered and outgunned in the battle, praise God. When you are desperate, praise God. If you are struggling with addictions, sin, fears, or confusion, praise God. If you feel ill or physically weak, praise God. If your heart is broken or you are battling worries and stress, praise God. If you feel depressed, discouraged, or even suicidal, praise God.

When you praise God, you are confronting strongholds. When you praise, you are addressing demonic powers. And whether they are emotional, mental, or spiritual, God will break them. Praise invites God into the situation.

It is my opinion that prophetic praise is warfare on a higher dimension of praise, and the victory we receive happens on a greater level!

> "As they began to sing and praise, the LORD set ambushes…"
>
> — 2 Chronicles 20:22 (NIV)

The Hebrew word for "began" is *chalal*. At the very first moment of their praise, God stepped in. At the beginning point of their song, the first line, first stanza, and first few notes, God stepped in. God did not wait for the whole song or for the entire dance routine or the whole worship session. God stepped in when they began. In the same way that they did not wait for the evidence to praise, God did not delay stepping in to give the victory.

God works through a process, and God does call us to a waiting time. Some things take longer than expected. But God does do sudden miracles! God does do things immediately! God also gives us breakthroughs and miracles right from the get-go. We cannot put God in a box or limit Him to a specific method or timetable. God does what He wants to do and when He wants to. Our part is to stay faithful and to always trust in God's ways and in His timing.

Praise is powerful. We need to praise God for all that He has done in our lives. We also need to prophetically praise God before He does what we have prayed about. Prophetically praise God based on the promises in His Word.

The Hebrew word for "began" is *chalal*. It is a complex Hebrew word. It does mean "beginning point," but it has another level of meaning that I love. It also means "to fatally wound, bore through, pierce, to lay open, to give access, and to perforate." Glory!

More than a starting point, when they began their praise, it created an access into the ranks of the enemy. When they started to praise God, it opened a gap and cut through the defenses of the enemy. When you start to praise before your miracle, there is a breaking into the enemy's camp and a breaking through the ranks of the enemy! Don't wait till you get your blessing to praise God; praise Him before you get your breakthrough. It may accelerate your miracle!

Application #3—Pre-prophetic Praise Posture

Prophetic praise is praising God for what has not yet happened based on what His Word says is possible. Prophetic praise happens in a context. The pre-prophetic praise phase is important preparation. Prophetic praise is facilitated by the pre-prophetic phase.

Prayer

The first thing they did was to pray and fast. It speaks of a relationship with God. That means spending time talking to God. It means getting into the Word and being a part of the Christian community. A relationship with God awakens the prophetic praise within us. True praise is born within the context of that relationship. A lifestyle of prayer unlocks the prophetic praise within us.

Place

God told them that He would fight their battle. In other words, God was stepping onto their battlefield. Then He asked them to show up there too! The right place matters! I am talking about being in the place where God is. We know that God is all over the world because He is omnipresent. But there are certain designated places where He calls us to gather together. I am not talking about a geolocation or a physical place. I am talking about a spirit location.

> "For where two or three gather in my name, there am I with them."
> — Matthew 18:20 (NIV)

> Not giving up meeting together, as some are in the habit of doing…
> — Hebrews 10:25 (NIV)

The battlefield was the designated place where God was going to show up. God said, "I will fight your battle," so they showed up. If you show up in the holy places of prayer and worship, in the holy places that are lifting up the Word of God, your praise will reach new levels. If you will commit to getting there, that is where the atmosphere is right to unlock the prophetic praise.

Posture

> "You will not have to fight this battle. Take up your positions; stand firm and see the deliverance the LORD will give you…"
>
> — 2 Chronicles 20:17 (NIV)

I want to share a quick note about the Hebrew word *'amad*. It means "to stand in your position, to present yourself upright and firm." It also means "to be in a standing attitude." We get the sense that God was saying to them, "Stand up straight, not bowed down or with your face in the mud." God was asking them to show up with a confidence in Him.

I stand with an attitude of strength, power, and peace because God's got my back. Not depressed, discouraged, disappointed, fearful, or terrified. A standing attitude says, "I resist you, devil; I defy you in Jesus' name." A standing attitude is knowing that although you are surrounded, God is with you. A standing attitude is, "Despite the way it looks, I still have hope." A standing attitude is, "I refuse to lie down and die."

Standing attitude is this, "I may not look like it, but I am an overcomer and more than a conqueror."

My dad, on his death bed, had an oxygen mask on, and he was on strong medication, and his left arm was swollen because of the IV drips. But when we prayed and praised God in the hospital room, He would pump his right fist in the air. On his death bed, he had a standing attitude. He died with a standing attitude! He did not lose because absent from the body is present with the Lord! We did not see him healed, but he got his healing in heaven.

Prophetic praise does not happen by accident. It is intentional.

CHAPTER EIGHT
Fake Deal or No Deal?

Counterfeits and scams seem to be the order of our day. There are so many scam calls and e-mails trying to take advantage of people. When we moved to Queens, New York, we initially did not have a car. The people from our congregation were amazing in how they drove us back and forth to services. Of course, the public transport in NYC is great, and people can survive without a car. We got to the place where we could afford to buy a car, and so we went around to local second-hand car dealers. And that turned out to be quite an adventure.

I finally discovered why second-hand car salesman is seen as symbolic of dishonesty and being unreliable. I also found out what "bait and switch" meant. We would see adverts in the newspaper or online for amazing deals and be the first people at the car dealerships the next morning, only to be told that those cars were sold. And that happened countless times until we realized the truth of those adverts. They were fake. Those cars did not exist! When we were told that they were sold, we were offered other "deals." Of course, nothing was as good as the fake deal. Either it was out of our price range, or the car was not in a very good condition.

One car dealer took me (and a few others) to an auction in Pennsylvania. We were advised that after buying a car, we should be prepared to spend at least a thousand dollars to make it roadworthy. On one occasion, we paid a deposit of five hundred dollars, but when we went to pick up the car, it was sold. The manager initially refused to return our deposit. It took several weeks to get back our money.

Apart from the lies and traps of the second-hand car salesman, we had some major obstacles against us. We had a very limited budget. And we were new immigrants with no credit history. And the search went on for a few months, and it was really frustrating and discouraging. This is no exaggeration; we probably looked at over one thousand cars. Did I mention that people from our church drove us back and forth to the car dealerships?

We did eventually buy a car. We actually bought a brand-new car. That was because our family friend from Pennsylvania cosigned the deal. In fact, he negotiated the deal, and all I had to do was take a bus to Redding, Pennsylvania (about three hours away), sign on the dotted line, and drive home with a brand new car. We are forever grateful to our friends, Mahen and Prash. There is so much I can say about our experiences, but that would need to be a book by itself.

So many times during our search for a car, I was tempted to just take the deal with the junky car because, in my mind, something was better than nothing. The longer a battle goes on, the more tempted we are to accept a deal to put an end to the battle. The devil is a master strategist at offering counterfeit deals. Sadly many lives have been ruined by his false deals. And others have missed out on the better things God had in store for them because they settled for the lesser options.

We are no ordinary prey; we do not have to settle for second best. I love the tagline for the reality show *Survivor*. It says, "Outwit. Outplay. Outlast." We have to train ourselves to fight to the final bell. Don't quit until you get the victory. "Something is better than nothing" is a lie from the devil. Jesus Christ did not die on the cross just so we would settle for whatever scraps the devil chooses to give to us. Jesus paid the price that we may have full, complete, and total victory.

There is a powerful lesson on the devil's deals in the Exodus story. Let me share a few lessons.

> And Moses said to the people, "Do not be afraid. Stand still, and see the salvation of the LORD, which He will accomplish for you today. For the Egyptians whom you see today, you shall see again no more forever. The LORD will fight for you, and you shall hold your peace."
>
> …Then Moses stretched out his hand over the sea; and the LORD caused the sea to go *back* by a strong east wind all that night, and made the sea into dry *land,* and the waters were divided. 22 So the children of Israel went into the midst of the sea on the dry *ground,* and the waters *were* a wall to them on their right hand and on their left.
>
> …Moses stretched out his hand over the sea, and at daybreak the sea went back to its place. The Egyptians were fleeing toward it, and the Lord swept them into the sea. The water flowed back and covered the chariots and horsemen—the entire army of Pharaoh that had followed the Israelites into the sea. Not one of them survived.
>
> — Exodus 14:13–14, 21–22, 27–28 (NIV)

This was God's plan: Israel walking to freedom through the Red Sea on dry ground. This was God's plan: Israel's enemies drowned in the Red Sea. This was God's plan: total freedom. This was God's plan: complete victory over their enemies. What an awesome miracle!

Their freedom started with Moses and Aaron confronting Pharaoh with the words, "Let my people go!" But before he let them go, he refused to let them go. But before they got to the Red Sea, they were in an intense battle. Their enemy, Pharaoh, came at them with counterfeit offers.

Pharaoh is a type of devil. When Satan has control over a life or situation, he does not easily let go. He keeps fighting over that territory or person. Pharaoh took a beating with the first nine plagues, but he kept resisting God's plan. He was still arrogant and stubborn. That is how Satan operates. Pharaoh played mind games. He told Moses that they could leave and then changed his mind. He did this over and over again. Satan plays games. He gives people the sense of freedom when they are not really free. The cycle goes on and on.

Pharoah's Deals

The plagues hit Pharaoh hard, so he started to alter his position. Pharaoh started to negotiate. But it was all just smoke and mirrors as he tried to get Moses to adjust his demands. He attempted to force Moses to compromise his position and back down and settle for second best. But the deals were intended to subvert God's original plan. That is just what Satan does; he offers counterproposals to God's plan. He plies us with his substitutes. When we accept, it is not just settling for second best; it is choosing the satanic option.

Pharaoh offered Moses three deals. I want to place them into three major categories, Faith Foundations, Family, and Finances.

Deal #1: Faith Foundations

Then Pharaoh summoned Moses and Aaron and said, "Go, sacrifice to your God here in the land."

...Pharaoh said, "I will let you go to offer sacrifices to the LORD your God in the wilderness, but you must not go very far."

— Exodus 8:25, 28 (NIV)

At first, Pharaoh rejected Moses' request to allow Israel to go off and worship the Lord. Then he agreed, but it was a conditional offer. Moses asked for a three-day journey out of Egypt, but Pharaoh offered worship in Egypt. In this context, Egypt is symbolic of a place that Satan controls. I interpret this compromise offer from Pharaoh as, "Worship on a foundation where I am still king and lord and master."

I define an "ungodly foundation" as "anything that violates the Word of God." Can I just say it like it is? We are living in a time when so many Christians are compromising on the foundations of our faith. Too many Christians have settled for the counterfeit. Too many Christians are happy with satanic substitutes. The devil doesn't mind Christians who have settled for compromising and contaminated faith foundations. They are no threat to the kingdom of darkness. They are not faithful representatives of the gospel. The devil is not bothered by those who claim to be Christians but have not made Jesus their Lord and Savior. Instead of the church being a world-changer, the world is influencing the church.

Our faith foundations are holy. And whatever we do to practice our faith (worship, pray, study the Word of God, etc.), that location becomes holy ground, and that atmosphere is anointed. We refuse to settle for anything less.

We are no ordinary prey; we need to rise up and fight against those things that try to contaminate or control our worship. We are no ordinary prey; we do not settle for giving God lip service, drawing near with our words when our hearts are far from God. We are no ordinary prey; we do not settle for a compartmentalized one hour on a Sunday morning worship. We are no ordinary prey; we do not settle for an online worship service when it is possible for us to worship in person in the house of God with the people of God. And of course, this does not apply to those who have physical and health challenges.

We have been called to worship God in spirit and in truth. We have been created to worship God with all our hearts, minds, souls, and spirits, with all our strength. We have been called to a lifestyle of worship.

Deal #2: Family

> Pharaoh said, "The LORD be with you—if I let you go, along with your women and children! Clearly you are bent on evil. No! Have only the men go and worship the LORD, since that's what you have been asking for."
>
> — Exodus 10:10–11 (NIV)

The second deal Pharaoh offered was this: that only the men could attend this worship service. This represents an attack on the family. Pharaoh wanted to divide the family in their worship. We know that the family is the devil's favorite target. So many families are divided in their faith. In many families, only one person in the home is serving God, while the rest of the family is unconcerned about spiritual matters. We know that one person can and does make a difference to the rest of the family, but it is so much more powerful when all agree on Jesus Christ as Lord.

Pharaoh knew that even if the men went to worship, they would have to come back for their wives and children. As long as he controlled the home base, he had the upper hand. We are God's people, and that means we are no ordinary prey. We refuse that the devil has any control over our families. We refuse to give the devil room in our family life. We need to fight for our families.

It is not okay that some members of the household are unconcerned about spiritual matters. So we will pray until that changes. It is not okay that some family members have no prayer life. We will take a hold of God and not let go until that changes. It is not okay that some family members will not go to church. And we will not settle for that option. We will fight through until the words of Joshua are true over our families too, "…as for me and my house, we will serve the Lord" (Joshua 24:15, NIV). We are no ordinary prey, and so our goal must be no family member left behind.

Deal #3: Finances

> Then Pharaoh summoned Moses and said, "Go, worship the LORD. Even your women and children may go with you; only leave your flocks and herds behind."
>
> — Exodus 10:24 (NIV)

The third deal was to take the women and the children but leave their stuff behind. Pharaoh wanted them to worship God empty-handed. In the Old Testament, worship meant bringing an offering of lambs, bulls, fruits of crops, etc. Worship meant a sacrifice to God. Pharaoh's deal called for worshipping God without giving Him anything.

Very often, people are tied to their stuff. A rich young man came to Jesus, and he bragged about how he followed everything in the law and then asked Jesus, "What more can I do?" Jesus said, "Sell all and give it to the poor and follow me." But he could not do it. The Bible says, "For where your treasure is, there your heart will be also" (Matthew 6:21, NIV). We cannot serve both God and our money or possessions. People are afraid to give to God their tithes and offerings, their time, talents, or ability. Don't let your finances determine the level of your worship.

Each time, Moses rejected the deals that Pharaoh offered him. Finally, God breaks Pharaoh with the tenth plague. Israel is set free on the night of the Passover.

On the Brink of a Breakthrough

We do get weary, and sometimes we are tempted to give in to the counterfeit offer of the devil. We get frustrated, and sometimes we think something is better than nothing. Take note of this; it was just after Pharaoh's final deal; God said to Moses that He would send one more plague, the tenth. Don't give up because you never know how close you are to your breakthrough. The tenth plague broke Pharaoh, and Israel left Egypt.

Going Out of Business Deals

Even after we say no to the devil's counterfeits, he will still come after us. We need to stay committed to the Word of God.

> When an impure spirit comes out of a person, it goes through arid places seeking rest and does not find it. Then it says, "I will return to the house I left." When it arrives, it finds the house swept clean and put in order. Then it goes and takes seven other spirits more wicked than itself, and they go in and live there. And the final condition of that person is worse than the first.
>
> — Luke 11:24–26 (NIV)

Even after being cast out, the devil comes back to check out the person. Then he attempts to get back into the very person he was cast out of. We have a relentless enemy. Even after he is defeated, he comes back.

In Luke 4:13 (NIV), Jesus was on a forty-day fast. Jesus defeated Satan when he tried to tempt Him.

> "When the devil had finished all this tempting, he left him until an opportune time."

The King James Version says, "He left Him for a season." In other words, he planned to get back at Jesus at another appropriate time. This is Jesus we are talking about—the Messiah, the Christ, the Son of God. The devil is a determined foe. Pharaoh was still trying to hold on to Israel after the devastating losses. It makes no sense. That is the nature of the beast we are up against. He is always chasing after those who are free. He is always pursuing those who have been set free, trying to regain control over them.

The enemy of our souls works in various ways. Here are a few of his strategies.

The devil will use generational issues to tell us that we are no better than the history of our family. And the goal is that we should settle for that level of faith or lack of faithfulness. We are no ordinary prey; we do not have to be weak Christians like our families may have been.

The past is one of the biggest hooks that the enemy tries against us. He tries to convince us that we will always be who we used to be. The devil glamorizes the past. Everything was the "good old days." The truth is that life was not as perfect as we think it was. When the going gets tough, many people often run back to who they used to be. I am no ordinary prey; the past is over, and I am a new creation in Christ Jesus.

We refuse to let our problems or pain determine the level of our faith or contaminate our worship. We refuse to let people and the trouble they try to cause in our lives set the tone for our love for God.

When You Refuse to Compromise

Moses and Israel said, "No deal" to Pharaoh. And God honored the stand that they took. God broke Egypt with the final plague. God protected them at the Red Sea when Pharaoh chased after them. And then God destroyed their enemies.

God can do that for us today if we are willing to stay true to Him. We need discernment to say no to the counterfeits of the devil.

When we take a stand for God, when we declare "No deal" to the counterfeits of the enemy, something will happen. God steps in. God steps in behind us. God closes the way behind us. Just like Israel had the cloud and God's angel behind them, God closes up the way behind you so the devil cannot touch you. He will try, but he cannot lay a hand on God. He has to back up. Generational issues will come at you, trying to force you to go backward, but God has got your back. The past will chase you; problems and pain will come against you, trying to stop your spiritual growth, but God has got your back. Problem people will try to knock you off balance, but God has got your back.

We are no ordinary prey; by the grace of God, we don't have to accept the devil's deals. Amen!

CHAPTER NINE
Put the Pedal to the Metal

I have always loved to drive fast. I have had some incredibly fast journeys while driving or as a passenger with my friends. Unfortunately for drivers like me, the traffic police in our little town was quite passionate about their jobs. One of their favorite traps was to hide in the bushes and then jump out and pull over those drivers that were speeding. They used handheld radars, and back then, no one questioned the validity of those devices. There was one traffic officer who rode about on a motorbike who was especially disliked by many people because he handed out a lot of traffic fines. I remember a time when he was chasing me, and I got away from him. Because at the time, I was an unlicensed seventeen-year-old driving my mom's car.

Fast drivers will tell you that one of the most frustrating things on the road is when you are behind a slow-moving vehicle or stuck in heavy traffic. And on our streets in Staten Island, it seems like there is a speed camera on every block.

Have you noticed how in life and in ministry, there are so many things that come to slow us down? At one moment, we could be soaring with wings like eagles, just loving God and enjoying life, and then without warning, it seems like we come to a standstill. And it seems like there is always one thing after another that comes to slow us down. Let me share a story about a journey that our family made several years ago and then a few lessons to motivate us that we are no ordinary prey.

Cape Town Drive

Many years ago, Valerie and I took a road trip to Cape Town with our two-year-old daughter, Kimberly. The drive from Durban was about 1600 kilometers (almost 1000 miles). We drove for over two days.

Obstacles

We set off very early in the morning, so we had the advantage of quiet roads. The three-lane highways were in excellent condition. At an average speed of 170 kilometers per hour (106 miles/hr), we made great progress. That was until we reached a part of the journey through the Transkei. Transkei was an independent country within the borders of South Africa that was created by the Apartheid government. But that is a story for another time.

When we reached Transkei, it totally changed our journey. Firstly, it brought an end to the three-lane highway. It was all single-lane roads. The roads were narrow, and on either side of the road, there were houses. Houses meant people and children. That meant the hazard of people running across the street without warning. There were innumerable potholes. It looked a lot like our roads in New York City after a severe winter.

The biggest surprise was the animals. There were farms along the way, and most of the farms had no fences or broken fences. So there were cattle grazing along the roadside, and of course, they would wander onto the road. These included cattle, goats, horses, sheep, and even pigs.

Speeding along at a hundred miles per hour was impossible. Apart from the potholes, I had to be on the lookout for animals. Cows crossing the road had no interest in the traffic or in the rules of the road. They did not even respond to honking. It was both frustrating and dangerous. Just as the danger posed by knocking into a deer, we heard of many cars being damaged and people being hurt when they knocked into the farm animals. Many times I had to come to a complete standstill. This went on for hundreds of miles.

But there was another factor on these roads, and that was the trucks. Those trucks were unlike the eighteen wheelers that we see on our interstate. Our trucks are fast, but the ones on the Transkei roads were carrying heavy loads and moving very slowly. Whenever I came up behind a truck, I would look for a gap to overtake the trucks. That was not always easy because of the many hills and blind spots. Overtaking was problematic.

When I overtook a truck, I had such a sense of relief. I could put my foot down on the accelerator. But just as quickly as the truck was out of sight in my rearview mirror, another one would be up ahead of me. Sometimes the trucks were not traveling alone but had a trail of cars following them. Sometimes they would be crawling at 30 mph.

This obviously created an unimaginable delay because I had to wait until the cars passed the trucks. It was only then I had the opportunity to overtake the trucks. Unfortunately, not all drivers are created equal! Some drivers missed opportunities to pass the trucks because they were too slow or not willing to take the opportunity. *I think some of them were just there to frustrate me!*

There were times when I had to overtake a bunch of cars behind the truck and the truck in one move. That was not always the wisest thing to do, especially with pigs that could be crossing the street! As I got through one line of cars and trucks, I would come up behind another and another and another.

Did I mention the weather? As they say in Brooklyn, "Fuhged-daboudit." Then there was tiredness because I was driving a stick shift car. If you have ever driven a stick shift in heavy traffic, then you know that it is quite a workout. I also remember that there was a moment when my eyes closed for a few seconds because I was sleepy. All in all, this section of our trip was a workout on many levels.

Spiritual Life

I heard the Lord say to me, "The Christian life is like your journey through the Transkei." This is a way of life in which you will encounter obstacles and face situations that will slow you down. One moment, you may be on the move for God, enjoying new levels in the anointing and climbing higher spiritually. It may be smooth sailing. And suddenly, you are slowed down. Jammed at a slow pace and maybe even brought to a standstill. There are many things in life that can slow us down or bring us to a halt. Some of those challenges that can slow us down are negative thoughts and emotions. Others are painful experiences, setbacks, and failures. And, of course, there is the devil, a real enemy. He is always looking to disrupt our spiritual progress. He is a master at disruption. He is skilled in delaying tactics like discouragements and disappointments. Moreover, he is an expert in providing detours that will take us out of God's path for our lives. The bottom line is that there are many things in life that can slow us down. There are things in life that seek to dominate us, control us, and manipulate us.

This Christian life is like a road through Transkei filled with potholes. That is something those of us who live in New York

City know very well. Some potholes we create for ourselves; others the devil puts there. Sadly, those who are weak in their faith walk away from God in such moments. They return to their old lifestyle, turning their backs on Jesus Christ.

Christianity is not a smooth road. In fact, very often, it is not even a paved road. Very seldom is it a three-lane freeway. Jesus warned us in John 15:18 (NIV) when He said, "If the world hates you—remember it hated me before it hated you."

The Pharisees plotted against Jesus. They even accused Him of using demonic power to perform His miracles. They tried to undermine His ministry by challenging His words. They rejected Him. One of His disciples betrayed Him. If it happened to Jesus, it might very well happen to us.

In the book of Acts, we read about the amazing supernatural happenings. But we also read about the persecution against the church. The Old Testament prophets declared powerful words from God. They, too, had to deal with rejection and persecution.

Have you ever gone from revival to stand still? Have you ever gone from fresh fire to being burnt out? Have you ever gone from the mountain top to the valley in one day? Then you know what I am talking about. I am not saying that this way of life is like a roller coaster. I am not trying to paint a negative picture of Christianity. But I am saying to you that this is a tough path to walk. Especially if you want to be true to what Jesus taught. Daily we are faced with oppositions and attacks. They have one aim, to slow us down or, if possible, to stop us altogether. The devil seeks to frustrate us. He wants us to give up hope. He wants to make us feel that God does not care.

Application

When we encountered a slow-moving truck ahead of us, the natural reaction was one of frustration, irritation, and even anger. I was hot and bothered. When we passed a truck, there was another one that was further down the road. Just when you have dealt with one situation, there is another waiting down the road. It may not look the same, but the intention is the same, that is, to slow you down and to bring you to a halt. Just when you conquer one mountain, you will meet another. Just when you have overcome one challenge, you will face another along the way. Sometimes it will feel like there is one thing after another that you have to deal with. Sometimes you may have to deal with challenging situations many times in one day.

We made it to Cape Town. We, too, will make it on this journey with God. Here are some lessons to encourage remembering that we are no ordinary prey.

Keep the destination in mind

When we came up behind a truck or slow-moving car, we did not pull over and cry. Neither did we make a U-turn and go back home. Cape Town was at the back of our minds. Cape Town is one of the most beautiful cities in the world. We were thinking about visiting the southernmost tip of the African continent. We were focusing on seeing the place where the two oceans, the Atlantic and the Indian, meet. We were looking forward to going to Robben Island, where Mandela was in prison, and getting to the top of Table Mountain. So we stayed on the road despite the obstacles.

Do not give up on the journey with Christ. Keep the goal in mind. The goal is heaven, our eternal destination. When the situations of life slow you down, do not quit. Heaven is worth any and every amount of suffering you may have in this life. Stay on the path with Jesus. Do not turn back. We have to recognize that in this way of life, there are things that can slow us down. Behind the obstacles and hurdles, behind the traps and temptations, are the plots and plans of Satan. There is a hidden agenda, so stay determined. Tell yourself, "I am going to get beyond this because I am going somewhere." With that attitude, the devil will know that you are no ordinary prey!

Holiness

I overtook trucks, and at times I passed several cars at once. But I was not reckless. My wife and our two-year-old daughter were in the car with me. I drove carefully. Do not compromise your holiness in tough times. Holiness will keep you safe. When tough times come, that is when Satan will tempt us to be reckless. If we take it his way, it can kill us—literally and spiritually. Holiness is a powerful safeguard. Holiness is a loud and clear message that we are no ordinary prey.

Patience

I needed patience on that road through the Transkei. There were times when the road had lots of winding bends. That made it difficult for me to pass the trucks. At other times, the cows and pigs blocked the way, and they were in no hurry to cross the street. It called for a lot of patience. The Bible says that he who endures to the end shall be saved. We have to be committed to outlasting the devil. Satan threw everything he could against Job, but Job held on, and Job came through. The Bible has numerous examples of people who outlasted the assignments of the devil, i.e., Joseph, David, and Mordecai.

I also needed patience because it was unfamiliar territory for me. I needed patience because the roads were windy and narrow. I needed patience because there were lots of potential hazards along the way. I needed patience because, at times, there were three or four trucks traveling one behind the other. When the opportunity arose, I passed them one by one. Patience will keep us moving forward. Patience is a powerful weapon against the devil.

Sensitive

Some cars seemed happy to be traveling behind the truck, but I was always looking for a gap to get ahead. Have you ever tried to pass a slow-moving car that would speed up as you tried to pass them? Some people just want us driving behind them! It is even harder when a long truck speeds up as you try to pass it.

I was not content to sit behind the trucks all the way to Cape Town. In this journey, slowing down may be unavoidable, and it is not wrong. But staying slowed down is wrong. Let me explain it this way. Life may throw things at you that can slow your spiritual progress. Don't let it control or dominate you. Look for ways to get beyond them. You should not live disappointed forever. You should not live in frustration forever. You should not live angry forever. You may have messed up, but do not live in that sin forever.

Look for ways to beat the thing that has slowed you down. The good news is that you don't have to do it alone. Seek godly help. Seek prayer. Talk to someone. Be spiritually sensitive. Sensitivity will enable you to overtake whatever the devil puts in front of you, and that lets the devil and his emissaries know that you are no ordinary prey.

Faith is action

It is not only seeing the gap to overtake but also taking the gap that is important. Many people know what they need to do to move along in their spiritual life, but they do not do anything about it. Faith is action. When we took the gap, the long truck or the slow-moving car was way behind us. We had an open road, and we were moving at a hundred miles an hour! Whenever you act in faith, God will reward your faith. You will be amazed at how God can come through for you if you act in faith. Knowledge about the Word of God without the corresponding obedience will not make a difference in our lives. Putting our faith into action makes us no ordinary prey.

Invest in power

We were driving a good car. It was almost brand new and in excellent condition. And it had plenty of horsepower. So whenever we came up behind a truck, we knew that we could overtake them. So we waited for the moment, and then we passed them.

We had the power to accelerate. The trucks were bigger than us, but what kept us going was the knowledge that we had the power to overtake them. There were times when the trucks blocked my view of the road ahead. We knew we had the power to overtake them. We were slowed down countless times, but we knew it would not last forever. It was a long journey, almost a thousand miles. When we passed the slow-moving trucks, it was as if they were never there. Of course, at times, I had swift victories. There were times when I could see the open road, and I overtook a truck or a slow-moving car without even slowing down.

Just imagine if I was on a bicycle or on a horse and carriage. We would have had very little chance of overtaking anything. But we had horsepower. We invested in power. We had fuel injection, power steering, air conditioning, etc. Our car was not meant to sit behind slow-moving trucks or vehicles for hundreds of miles. It had the power to do more. We had power. We had ability. We could go beyond slow-moving trucks and cars because we invested in power.

In this spiritual life, that is what we have to do, invest in power. The power of God will help you overcome the things that slow you down. How do we invest in spiritual power? Here are some of the ways, and there is no need to elaborate on each aspect. We invest time in prayer, the Word of God, worship, fasting, serving, fellowship, witnessing, obedience, etc.

Without God's power, you cannot get beyond Satan's slowing down tactics. In the natural, we overtook trucks. But in the spiritual, we can go through the obstacles. We can destroy the hurdles. We can crush the attacks of Satan. If Satan has slowed you down or has brought you to a standstill, today, you can start moving again. Today, you can overtake the things that are holding you back.

We are no ordinary prey. We may be slowed down. But we were not made to stay slowed down by the devil. We may fall or mess up, but we were not made to stay down. We have a God who gives us the power to move ahead. We are no ordinary prey. We have the power of the name of Jesus. We were not intended to sit in Satan's hindrances. We are no ordinary prey. We have the power of the blood of Jesus. We were not intended to be dominated by Satan's plans. We are no ordinary prey. We have the power of the Holy Spirit. We were not intended to be destroyed by the devil's traps. We are no ordinary prey. We have the power of the Word of God. We were not intended to live in defeat, discouragement, or frustration.

God has invested power in us. Get up and use that power within you so that you may move ahead of whatever is trying to slow you down spiritually. On this journey, we have the power to overtake and overcome. Hallelujah!

Forewarned

Before we left for Cape Town, we were warned about the conditions through the Transkei area. People who had done the trip before us gave us valuable information. So when we saw the cows and pigs, we had already heard about them. When we came up behind slow-moving trucks, we had already heard about them. Having been forewarned, we took in our stride.

The Bible gives us valuable warnings about the days we are living in. So live with hope. It is the "last days," and some things are expected to happen. Do not fall apart. Others have walked this way before us. They made it, and so can we. God is in control. When we face challenges, it does not mean that God does not love us. Invest in spiritual power. Remember, as a child of God, He has invested in you. We can overcome the thing that tries to slow us down or stop us from moving forward with the Lord. We are no ordinary prey.

Here is what Jesus said to us in John 16:33 (NIV):

> "I have told you these things, so that in me you may have peace. In this world you will have trouble. But take heart! I have overcome the world."

Finally

The things that slowed us down through the Transkei kept coming up every few miles. Just when we got through one obstacle, there was another down the road. And just when I got past one slow-moving vehicle, I had to do it all over again.

That is how this life may be at times. Here is the key to overcoming the obstacles and attacks that will come your way—do it again. Do it again.

And then do it again. We are no ordinary prey. Amen.

CHAPTER TEN
Fight for Your Family

Family is the cause of a lot of heartache in the world. I must confess that during my wild teenage years, I gave my parents more than their fair share of heartache. Of course, I did not realize it at the time because I was so caught up with my lifestyle and my friends. There were countless occasions when I would drive home drunk after a party. Other times, I would pick fights with people who were much bigger and stronger than me. That I was not arrested or badly beaten was nothing short of a miracle. I realize now that it was the grace of God protecting me. And that grace was over my life because I had praying parents, especially a praying mom.

I want to share one particularly frightening experience and how my mom's prayers for me rescued me. I was carjacked in my mom's car. Everything about that moment was wrong. I was in the wrong place at the wrong time, obviously doing the wrong thing. The carjackers shoved me down into the backseat and drove off. They stopped in a deserted field and stripped me of my clothes. One of them threw me onto the ground and had a knife at my back. I fully expected to die that day. I remember crying out to God for mercy. Actually, I was saying things like, "Lord, please receive my soul into heaven." Of course, at that point in my life, I had drifted so far away from God. As I lay face down in the ground, I could hear my mom's voice praying for me. The hijacker who had me pinned down suddenly let me go, and they drove off. I probably walked over five miles barefoot through the bush to get to the highway. I had never walked barefoot anywhere, not even in my own home! Thankfully, a car stopped, and the driver gave me a ride home. I was about ten miles from home. I could not believe that I had made it out of that situation alive. In addition to that miracle, my mom's car was found intact the next day. Usually, cars that are stolen are chopped up for parts or burned. I went with the police to the place where the car was found, and I got in and drove the car home. The car did need a good cleaning.

I know this without any shadow of a doubt: that it was my mom's prayers that rescued me that day. There was nothing about the way I was living my life that deserved God stepping in to save me. I should have died and gone to hell that day. But God heard the cries of my mother and saved me. That's amazing grace. And that is the story of my life. A short time after that, I got radically saved.

I am grateful to God that my mom never gave up praying for me. Your prayers for your family make an awesome difference. Don't stop praying for them. At the right time, God will step in and rescue them because you prayed for them.

Our Society

It is my conviction that we are living in a society that is intentionally creating interference in family relationships. There is a demonic assignment to disrupt families. There is an increasing disconnection between parents and children. Sons and daughters are being cut off from their generational blessings. There is an exponential increase in the number of prodigal children in our world. And the division and estrangement between siblings have also reached unprecedented levels. And this is prevalent in Christian families and even in pastors' families too.

But the culture and the spirit of the world do not have to have the final say over our families and their future. We are no ordinary prey, and when the devil comes after our families, we need to make sure we don't let him get away with it and make him regret he ever looked in our direction!

The reason that I include this section in the book is that God works generationally. And as much as we need to fight for ourselves, we need to fight for our families too. When God told King Hezekiah of the disaster coming to the nation of Judah in the future, Hezekiah was glad that it would not happen in his lifetime. That was a wrong attitude. We see the results of that in Hezekiah's son, King Manasseh. Because of his wickedness, he was almost single-handedly responsible for the Babylonian exile. God said that he would have canceled the exile, except for Manasseh's wickedness.

Unreachable Family

More often than not, the people in families that are under the attack of the devil are unreachable.

Physical

The most obvious reason that we cannot reach those family members under attack is because of the physical distance. Today, many families are scattered all over the world. Sometimes because of the distance, we are unaware of the trouble they are dealings with.

Emotional

Sometimes we are unable to reach people because of the emotional disconnect. Sometimes family may be within our physical reach, but they may want to have nothing to do with us, or they may not want to hear us out.

Hard Ground

There may be times when our family will "yes" us to death. They will show up, talk to us, and even listen to us or pretend to listen to us, but they are receiving nothing from us.

Demonic

Then there are times when our family is closed off to us because of a demonic blockage. The Bible clearly says that the devil comes to steal the Word and that he blinds the hearts and minds of people so they cannot see the truth. And the devil can and does use people to hinder our relationship and influence over family members, especially children.

Pain

There is deep pain when we cannot reach the ones we love and when we cannot get through to them. There are so many families that are heartbroken. And no matter what we do, it falls on deaf ears. In those moments, we do feel powerless and helpless. In those moments, fear, stress, and anger can overwhelm us. To be brutally honest, when things are out of our control, our faith is seriously challenged because we wonder why God would allow this to happen under our roof.

Valerie and I were praying on the phone with some friends across the miles and oceans. Our friends and prayer partners, Pastor Paul and Lucy Pillay (Nazareth Family Church, Chatsworth, Durban), prayed this line that God can reach people anywhere. Here is the truth; distance is not an issue to our God, whether it is physical or emotional.

> Surely the arm of the LORD is not too short to save,
> nor his ear too dull to hear.
>
> — Isaiah 59:1 (NIV)

I want to encourage you today that God can reach your unreachable families that are under attack from the devil. God can reach your family members who feel unworthy, unloved, or even angry at you and angry at God. God can reach in and deliver them from their dark places. God can break chains and shackles and destroy curses and generational curses. God can touch them and cut off the access the devil has to their lives. God can make them whole again.

Abraham and Lot

A powerful example of prayer for our families is the story of Abraham praying for his nephew Lot. When Abraham traveled out of his homeland in obedience to the call of God, his nephew Lot went with him. Lot's father had died, and Abraham probably felt responsible for him. Abraham had no children, so it is likely that he could have viewed his nephew as a son and potential heir.

However, they got to the point when they had to separate. The problems arose because their servants quarreled among themselves. They got so wealthy that the land could not support both of them. Abraham suggested a way out.

> So Abram said to Lot, "Let's not have any quarrel-
> ing between you and me, or between your herders
> and mine, for we are close relatives. Is not the whole
> land before you? Let's part company. If you go to the
> left, I'll go to the right; if you go to the right, I'll go
> to the left."
>
> — Genesis 13:8–9 (NIV)

My opinion is that Abraham had hoped that Lot would take ten steps to the left and he would take ten steps to the right and stop. I believe that Abraham wanted to be able to wave at Lot from his kitchen window or the second-floor balcony. Abraham may have wanted to be able to take a stroll and be at his nephew's house. But Lot had other plans. He saw land that looked like the garden of Eden, and he was hooked. Lot chose to settle close to Sodom. The Bible is clear that this was a wicked city.

Lot's Focus

> Abram dwelled in the land of Canaan, and Lot
> dwelled in the cities of the plain, and pitched his
> tent toward Sodom. But the men of Sodom were
> wicked and sinners before the LORD exceedingly.
>
> — Genesis 13:12–13 (NIV)

His tent was pitched towards Sodom, facing or focused on Sodom. This is more than a physical direction; it seems to indicate a direction of his heart, his soul's desire, an inner longing, and a spiritual choice. Eventually, Lot moved into the town. We see him settled in the town, and his daughters were engaged to local men. So Lot was happily going about his business in Sodom.

In Genesis 19:1, when the angels arrived, Lot was seated at the gates. In the Old Testament, the gates were a place of authority, where important decisions were made. Often it was the leaders and the influential men who sat at the gates. Lot was comfortably seated at the gates. That says that he was one of the key leaders of the city. He was one of the decision-makers, key players, and a part of the movers and shakers of the town. Can we say that he was a big boy in Sodom? Lot was no longer a newcomer or an outsider.

Lot may not have liked everything going on in Sodom, and he may not have approved of everything, but he made a choice to settle down. So many people turn a blind eye to things they do not approve of because they like where they are, because they have become comfortable and do not want to move again or give up their position. We know that people will compromise just to stay comfortable even when they know they are in the wrong place.

> With the coming of dawn, the angels urged Lot, saying, "Hurry! Take your wife and your two daughters who are here, or you will be swept away when the city is punished." When he hesitated, the men grasped his hand and the hands of his wife and of his two daughters and led them safely out of the city, for the Lord was merciful to them.
>
> — Genesis 19:15–16 (NIV)

The angel tells him to leave Sodom immediately, but he delays. The angels have to literally grab him by the hand and pull him out of there. Then God says, "Flee to the mountains," but he negotiates an easier option for himself. Despite Lot's shenanigans, God spares the city of Zoar for his sake.

> So when God destroyed the cities of the plain, he
> remembered Abraham, and he brought Lot out of
> the catastrophe that overthrew the cities where Lot
> had lived.
>   — Genesis 19:29 (NIV)

It was not about Lot. It was not about his wife or his daughters. It was Abraham's prayers for him that caused him to be rescued. That prayer is recorded in Genesis 18.

Although Lot had moved away, Abraham went to war when he was kidnapped. Abraham defeated four kings and their armies to rescue his nephew. We see a deep-rooted concern for Lot. But even after he was rescued, Lot went back to Sodom. He went right back to the danger zone. Some of you may be nodding your head because you have had this experience with your family members. But despite Lot moving away and choosing to stay away, Abraham never stopped praying for him or being concerned about Lot. God honored Abraham's heart for Lot. God rescued Lot out of Sodom's fire because Abraham was praying for him.

Application

The lesson is clear, never give up on praying for your loved ones. Even when they dismiss you or disrespect you, never give up on praying for them. Even when they disappoint you and bring shame and dishonor to your family, never give up on praying. And if they hurt you or break your heart, pray for them. They may not value themselves or even you, but never give up on praying for them.

Although Lot walked away from him, Abraham never stopped keeping watch over him. And what God did for Abraham, he can do for your family too. God can pull them out of the fire. God can step in just when they need it the most.

Your prayers are greater than their wicked choices and evil influences. Your prayers are greater than their sinful locations or their disrespect. Your prayers are greater than their sin. Your prayers in Jesus' name are greater than any and all demonic strongholds on their lives. Your voice and your influence may be silenced in their hearts, but your prayers will touch heaven on their behalf.

Our prayers become a covering for our family and friends. Our prayers release God's grace, mercy, help, protection, etc., into their lives. So keep praying. Keep praying when there are no results. Keep praying even when things go from bad to worse. You may be far away physically, but that cannot limit your prayers. You may be estranged; that too cannot limit your prayers. Their dislike and disrespect cannot limit your prayers.

God's Rescue in Motion

There may be times when God answers our prayers that it may feel like He did not. From Lot's point of view, his house was burning; his investments and wealth were being destroyed. All the stuff that he had built up over the years was going up in flames.

Abraham prayed for him, but he was losing so much. However, the greater blessing was happening. He was losing material stuff, but he was being rescued from brimstone and fire. Sometimes when we pray for people, it may actually seem like things are getting worse. I describe it as "God's rescue in motion." They may lose a job or a relationship, but that may be God's rescue in motion. God's rescue in motion may not always match our expectations or meet with our approval. We will never fully understand God or His Ways, and He will not necessarily go in the direction we expect Him to. God's rescue in motion may be confusing.

But God always knows how to get the job done. Sodom and its influence over Lot needed to be burned. Lot could have seen a house; God saw evil influences, curses, bondages, and strongholds. When God rescues people, He knows what or who they need to be delivered from. Some things need to go up in flames so there can be no return. Some bridges need to be burned so there can be no way back.

Because most people have a tendency to go backward rather than forward, most people have a tendency to cry for the past than look forward to the future. God's rescue in motion may not always look pretty. But having prayed, we need to trust God that He knows what He is doing.

Lot most likely knew that he was crossing a line moving into Sodom. It is my opinion that his wife and daughters were caught up in the lifestyle of the place. Lot could have known about his daughters and his wife's illicit activities. But he never asked Abraham for help, even though Abraham had rescued him when he was taken captive. Lot must have known that his uncle cared about him and loved him. Lot knew that Abraham would help him. But he did not ask for help. Most people do not freely ask for help because of their pride or sense of embarrassment.

So people behave as if all is well, wearing their masks of pretend perfection.

What people do after God has rescued them is their move. We can pray that the Lord will save them, deliver, and heal them. God does respond to such prayers. But they need to get to the place where they personalize their relationship with God. Salvation is a personal decision. Our prayers may rescue a person, but they will not save them and get them into heaven. Our prayers may get family members delivered from the clutches of Satan, but they will not get them into heaven. God's rescue should hopefully inspire them and motivate an awakening of their faith. Some people need multiple rescues before they change their lives. So keep praying.

We are no ordinary prey. Don't sit back and watch family drift away from God. Fight for them. God gave you to them because he knew that you would never give up on praying for them. Don't just pray casually, "God bless them." You go to war for them. You bind and cancel the works and the words of the devil over their lives. You shut down the influence and operation of the devil in their lives. Pray against witchcraft and sin. Pray against generational curses. Prophesy blessings into their lives. Ask God to send angels to war for them and to minister to them.

Like my story, there are countless people who made it because they had a praying family member.

CHAPTER ELEVEN
Start the War...
But Don't Tell Anyone

I have carried sermons inside me for years. And I waited for the right time to preach them. There were countless times that I was so thrilled with the revelation God gave me that I was ready to explode with them. But then I had to wait because it was not time. I had to wait because it was not the appointed place or not the designated people or not the right season for that word. That does not mean that I could not have preached that sermon anytime in any place to anyone. But the Holy Spirit was guiding me until I could hit the bull's eye with that word. Most pastors and preachers have similar stories to tell.

Guard what God says to you closely. The Lord said to Daniel, "...seal up the vision...it is not for now..." When God shows you something, don't rush off and broadcast it to the whole world. We need to be careful about the timing of what we share with others. We need to be careful with whom we share our dreams.

It is important to check that what God has revealed to you is for everyone, for some people, or just for you. People can steal your dreams and talk you out of God's purpose for your life. People can discourage or ridicule God's word or revelation to you. People can mock your faith in God. David was ready to take on Goliath, but his own brothers tried to put him off.

There are prayers that I pray that I share with no one. The reason for that is that not everyone is on the same level in their walk with God. I learned a long time ago that there are some things God allows me to see and hear because I am a pastor. And not everyone in the congregation will agree with how God leads me to pray over a particular situation. People may be thrilled by what they can see or hear, but they could be missing the heart of the matter. And there are times when the shining star is just the devil in camouflage.

Praying people hear and see things from God that others may not. Prophetic people hear and see things that not everyone can. So we have to be careful about what we share with others. And be careful with whom you share your heart or dreams or prayers.

I said all that to say this—the Lord may call us to go to war but to keep it close to the vest. God may want you to start a war against the devil's strongholds or operations privately. And the reason that God may give you an undercover operation could be that others are unwilling or unconcerned or just not as passionate as you are about that particular issue. Others may have become comfortable with something that makes your blood boil. So God may call you to start a war because of the level of your faith or the depth of your revelation and discernment.

You are going to love this lesson that I am going to share with you. This is one of my top ten favorite stories in the whole Bible. When I first preached this text, I titled the sermon "An Adventurous Anointing."

> Jonathan said to his young armor-bearer, "Come, let's go over to the outpost of those uncircumcised fellows. Perhaps the LORD will act in our behalf. Nothing can hinder the LORD from saving,

whether by many or by few." "Do all that you have in mind," his armor-bearer said. "Go ahead; I am with you heart and soul."

— 1 Samuel 14:6–7 (NIV)

In a nutshell, Israel was oppressed by the Philistines, who were the superpower of the day. Jonathan, the son of King Saul, rises up and starts a battle, which gains momentum and ends up being a great victory for Israel. There are some wonderful lessons for us in regards to being no ordinary prey.

Context of Israel's Situation

The Philistines were Israel's archenemies. There were constant struggles that took place between the two nations. Personally, I lay the blame at Samson's door. If he had done what he was born to do, he would have wiped out the Philistines. Instead, hundreds of years after his death, Israel continued to do battle with the Philistines. They oppressed Israel and often got the upper hand over them. This period was before David killed Goliath, so the Philistines were at the height of their power.

Israel was outnumbered and outgunned. To make matters worse, King Saul was disobedient to God. The prophet Samuel had already declared that God had taken away the kingdom from him.

Israel's Leadership

Saul was staying on the outskirts of Gibeah under a pomegranate tree in Migron.

— 1 Samuel 14:2 (NIV)

The Message (MSG) says it this way:

Meanwhile, Saul was taking it easy under the pomegranate tree at the threshing floor on the edge of town at Geba (Gibeah). There were about six hundred men with him.

King Saul was the leader of the nation. He was the commander in chief. He was the anointed king of Israel. Saul was the one the people were looking up to and ready to follow. Instead, he was on the outskirts or furthest away from the battle.

He is said to have been "under the tree" in the shade. The Message says, "…taking it easy…" There is a South African expression that ideally fits what he was doing; *he was parking in the shade*. He was in a safe, cozy place. Saul was a coward from day one. When they announced him as king, he was in hiding. Now even against the Philistines, he was in hiding. Saul had a modus operandi, and that was to hide away.

But Jonathan did not let his father stop him. He did not let his father's weakness become his weakness. He did not let his father's slackness become his slackness. He did not let his father's fear and doubts become his fears. He had a different heart, a different spirit, and a different mentality from his father. It is easy to blame leadership, parents, pastors, and others for anything and everything that goes wrong in our lives. Or you can arise and say, "It will not stop me."

First Samuel 14:3 (NIV) reveals that Jonathan did not tell anyone what he had planned and when and where he was going.

"…the people did not know he was gone…"

Obstacles

On each side of the pass that Jonathan intended to cross to reach the Philistine outpost was a cliff; one was called Bozez, and the other Seneh.

— 1 Samuel 14:4 (NIV)

There were steep rocks on the way forward. The rocks were named for a reason. There are no superfluous or irrelevant details in the Bible. It is my opinion that the names, places, sequence of events, etc., have a lesson to convey. In Hebrew, *Bozez* means "shining or whiter than white," while *Seneh* means "thorns."

The devil will try to block our progress and hold us back from going ahead for God. Here are two ways: shining, i.e., things that are attractive. The devil does come like "an angel of light." He makes sin attractive, but the end goal is to block our progress. Sometimes sin shines so brightly it can and does blind us to its dangers or creates blind spots. The thorns signify the trials, pains, or hurts in life. Those are things that can discourage us so that they stop us right in our tracks. The aim is to block our path.

Jesus is the way and the door. The devil is just the opposite. He is the obstacle, the blockage, and the hindrance. Those who seek to step out in faith need to be alert to the obstacles of the devil. Being alert requires discernment. The devil does not always look like we expect him to look or speak or appear. If we lack discernment, we can go from being adventurous in our faith to being trapped.

The Armor-Bearer

> Jonathan said to his young armor-bearer, "Come, let's go over to the outpost of those uncircumcised men. Perhaps the Lord will act in our behalf. Nothing can hinder the Lord from saving, whether by many or by few." "Do all that you have in mind," his armor-bearer said. "Go ahead; I am with you heart and soul."
>
> —1 Samuel 14:6–7 (NIV)

We have an armor-bearer, and He is the Holy Spirit. He is the One who is closest to us in the battle. He never leaves us nor forsakes us. If He left us for just one second, we would be destroyed. We are the royalty of God as royal priesthood. We are the special soldiers who serve in the army of God. We have an armor-bearer, and we do not enter into a battle alone. It is not by our own might or power; it is by the Spirit of the Lord. Isaiah 59:19 (KJV) says, "…the Spirit of the Lord will lift up a standard against him."

He brings the supplies that we need in the battle. The power we have is the Holy Spirit's power. The strength we have is the Holy Spirit's strength. The strategy we have is the Holy Spirit's strategy. Acts 17:28 (NIV) says, "…in Him we live and move and have our being." My armor-bearer is the Holy Spirit. He is ever-present.

Here is how I define radical Christianity in this context; it is those who will say, "Come with me, Holy Spirit." It is those who will say, "Back me up, Holy Spirit." The Bible says that we are led by the Spirit, and that is what I believe. But we do not need confirmation to pray for the sick. We do not need confirmation to counsel the abused or ask for deliverance. We do not need confirmation to reach out to the poor or evangelize the lost. It is already in the Word. Jonathan's move was faith in action. God wants such people today. If you believe that God can do it, go ahead, pray, and fast. If you believe that God is able, if you believe that God can do it, if you believe that God is bigger than the problem, if you believe that God is with you, then go ahead and exercise your faith. Go start a war. Become the catalyst for a victory. The enemy knows that catalysts are no ordinary prey.

The Results

> Jonathan climbed up, using his hands and feet, with his armor-bearer right behind him. The Philistines fell before Jonathan, and his armor-bearer followed and killed behind him.
>
> — 1 Samuel 14:13 (NIV)

God gave him a victory against all the odds, against a bigger and more powerful army.

> Then Saul and all his men assembled and went to the battle.
>
> — 1 Samuel 14:20 (NIV)

Others saw the battle, and they were encouraged to fight. The fearful joined in. Those who may be slack in their walk with God, doubtful, lukewarm, or in bondage will see the results of faith in action, and they will be inspired. They will be stirred up, and they too will join in the spiritual warfare. Catalysts inspire people to activate their faith.

> Those Hebrews who had previously been with the
> Philistines and had gone up with them to their
> camp went over to the Israelites who were with Saul
> and Jonathan.
>
> — 1 Samuel 14:21 (NIV)

The traitors and deserters who had joined forces with the enemy returned to fight for Israel. Backsliders will start serving God with a new zeal when they see the effects of our faith in action. Those who have turned their backs on Jesus will return to the fold. Others who call themselves Christians but are really enemies of the gospel will rise up in faith. All because they see the power of our radical faith in God.

> "When all the Israelites who had hidden in the hill
> country of Ephraim heard that the Philistines were
> on the run, they joined the battle in hot pursuit."
>
> — 1 Samuel 14:22 (NIV)

The people came out of hiding. The shy and embarrassed Christians will start to have an impact in their situation. Those hiding behind a million excuses for not serving God will be stirred up. Faith in action produces results. People will rise up and be on fire for God. Unexpected people enter the battle, and unlikely ones will become radical in their faith.

We may start off alone in the adventure, but we will get help from unexpected sources. David was alone when he went on the run from Saul, but before long, a powerful army assembled with him. You may feel afraid to take a stand because you think you cannot do it alone. Go ahead, take the stand, and watch what God will do.

Application

First Samuel 14:6 (NIV) is the key verse, "Nothing can hinder the Lord from saving, whether by many or by few." *We should make this the motto for our lives!* Here is the heart of a person who is no ordinary prey.

God is not limited by whether people have the ability or the necessary experience. God is not limited by whether people have the education or the good looks or the social status. It is not about our ability; it is about God! It is not about our resources; it is about God! All you need is confidence that God can! Go start a war in Jesus' name.

Others who should be engaged in spiritual warfare may lack the concern. Others who have the ability may not be interested in helping. Others that you thought you could count on may not be available. It may just be you and the Holy Spirit. But you and God are an awesome majority. Go start a war in Jesus' name. Let the devil know you are no ordinary prey.

Anytime you have a burden to see your family, friends, church, or nation blessed, you are on the right path. Go start a war in Jesus' name. Let the devil know you are no ordinary prey. The task may be great. The problems may be so deep. But God can do it through you. It is not about the size of the problem; it is about the greatness of our God. We need to shake off the feelings of inferiority and insecurity because our God is an awesome God. Go start a war in Jesus' name. Let the devil know you are no ordinary prey.

There are a lot of Christians who are very vocal about what they dislike in the world. There are a bunch of Christians who love making their opinions heard, even on social media. There are many Christians who are quick to pronounce judgment over things they dislike. And yet, no one will step up to the battlefield. All talk and no prayer! But when you start the war and God releases victory, those others will be inspired to get to the battlefield.

Concluding Note

A person who sees themselves as no ordinary prey is unafraid to declare, "Lord, You can do it, even if is it only me!" We need to get more militant and much bolder in our prayers. We need to get more aggressive in our warfare against the devil and his words and works.

Go start the war for your parents, your spouses, your children, and your friends. Go start the war for their healing, deliverance, marriage, health, finances, etc. Go start the war for your needs—emotional, relationships, career, studies, health, etc.

Go start the war by faith. God will back you up. God is not limited. God is always looking out for an adventurous person so that He can entrust the next move to them. Let the devil know you are no ordinary prey.

I do not want to be sitting in the shade in the back row; I want to be in the front row of God's army. I chose to step out of the back row mentality. I chose to step out of complacency, doubt, and fear.

We quote the verse, "The battle belongs to the Lord...," but we often don't get to the battlefield. In another battle, Saul and his army faced the Philistines, who had a giant on their team. Saul and the army must have been wondering, "Oh God, why don't You help us?" Look at the difference with David's approach, "David said to Saul, 'Let no one lose heart on account of this Philistine; your servant will go and fight him'" (1 Samuel 17:32). It was not David; it was neither the stones nor the sling that killed Goliath. It was David's no ordinary prey attitude and faith in God, "I come against you in the name of the Lord."

That line, "For the battle is not yours, but God's," is in the story of Jehoshaphat (2 Chronicles 20:15). He knew that God would fight for him, but he did not wait on the sidelines. He sent out the praise team, and they entered the battleground. God did the rest. Do something radical. Do something, do anything to let the devil know you are no ordinary prey!

Jonathan's name in Hebrew means "Jehovah has given." God has given you to your family. They may be difficult, but that is why God gave you to them. God has given you to your friendship circle. They may be untrustworthy, but that's why God gave you to them. God has given you to that company or business you work for. They may be rude, vulgar, or unethical, but that is why God gave you to them. God has given you to your church. They may have issues, but that is why God gave you to this church. God has given you to your community, your city, or your nation.

You are a God-given gift. God is awaiting you to step up and start the war. God will complete it. If you see a threat, deal with it. When the enemy threatens your home, family, marriage, health, business, job, or church, deal with it. Pray, "I come against you, Satan, in the name of Jesus. I bind your works by the blood of Jesus." Go start a war in Jesus' name. Let the devil know you are no ordinary prey.

The weapons of our warfare are not carnal. We have God's authority in the name of Jesus, the blood of Jesus Christ, the Word of God, and the Holy Spirit. Our God is not limited to whether He can save by many or by few.

CHAPTER TWELVE
Surviving the Detour

When I am driving, I prefer to take the easiest and straightest route to where I am going. Valerie, however, takes the scenic routes and the shortcuts. My choice is to have the least amount of twists and turns to get to the destination. When I go to the mall (rarely), I just have to drive down two major streets, Victory Boulevard, and then onto Richmond Avenue. Valerie usually takes a winding, single-lane route with many turns, while I drive on a road with four lanes. I would rather stay in heavy traffic than take shortcuts with many turns to get quicker to the destination.

Delays are hard to handle because we are so used to having things done immediately. Sometimes even the smallest delay can cause us to lose our composure. Have you noticed how delays often end up in detours? When we are faced with heavy traffic that is at a standstill, we look for exits and off-ramps to get off that road.

When we lived in Tennessee, we would get our food at the drive-thru window at fast food places and then take our daughter Kimberly inside to eat her happy meal and play on the indoor jungle gyms. We did this because the drive-thru was faster, and we probably saved a minute or two.

In a delay, we become vulnerable. Delays challenge us. They can even make us desperate or vicious. In a delay, some people are more open to trying almost anything to get out of it. In a delay, we are open to even bending the rules. When we are vulnerable, the devil comes looking for a gap. If we are spiritually weakened by the delay, Satan will take the gap. And the devil always has an agenda. So delays can put us on a detour, and some detours can take us far off track.

Attacking God's Purpose

Detours can carry a serious consequence because when we get detoured, it concerns God's purposes on the earth. God has purposes and plans for every person, and all of us have a blessing that we carry that we have been designed to release upon the earth. We have individual purposes that are unique and specialized. No one else can do what we have been created to do. And what we have been called to do is amazing because what happens in and through us is the work of the Holy Spirit.

> "For I know the plans I have for you," declares the
> Lord, "plans to prosper you and not to harm you,
> plans to give you hope and a future."
> — Jeremiah 29:11 (NIV)

These thoughts of our God to bless us are at a higher level than we can ever imagine.

> However, as it is written: "What no eye has seen,
> what no ear has heard, and what no human mind
> has conceived" the things God has prepared for
> those who love him.
> — 1 Corinthians 2:9 (NIV)

God wants to bless us at a level we cannot even think, dream of, or even imagine. God wants to bless us in ways we have never been blessed before. And God is able to do in and through us more than we even know is possible. But it is not always a smooth road to God's purpose because there is an enemy of our souls. The devil is the thief, and the devil will fight your purpose. And if the devil gets a foothold in a life, he brings chaos.

We are on the winning team. If God be for us, who can be against us? We are more than conquerors, and we are overcomers in Jesus Christ. And in the battle, we are victorious. No weapon formed against us will prosper, and no word against us will stand. The gates of hell will not prevail against the church. Hallelujah! We are on the winning side. We serve a mighty God, and we have a powerful purpose and calling.

But the enemy works to convince us that we are losing. And when we accept that lie, we surrender God's purpose for our lives. People sacrifice their faith. Others give up on their God-given callings and purpose. People walk away from the blessed life God promised. Not only does the enemy steal us away from God's purpose, but he also pushes a counterfeit in our face. Many times we choose the lesser thing instead of God's favor. When we take the counterfeit, the devil will keep pulling us deeper into the dark place. Some people get in so deep they can find it hard to believe God anymore. People get so lost they are convinced that it is over between them and God. Some feel that they have lost so much and are so far gone that there is no hope of getting back to God.

When you go through tough places that break you into a million pieces, it is easy to believe that it is all over for you, and it feels like you are a million miles away from God's plan.

Hagar

One of the most powerful couples in the Bible lost their way. A delay set up a detour, and it created an unthinkable mess. I'm referring to Abraham and Sarah.

> Now Sarai, Abram's wife, had borne him no
> children. But she had an Egyptian slave named
> Hagar; so she said to Abram, "The LORD has kept
> me from having children. Go, sleep with my slave;
> perhaps I can build a family through her." Abram
> agreed to what Sarai said.
>
> — Genesis 16:1–2 (NIV)

This power couple had a promise that God was going to bless them with a family and countless descendants. But time was running out, and God's plan seemed no closer to being fulfilled than when God first told them about it.

From the words of Sarai, we get the sense that she was blaming God. She says, "God did it to me." In other words, "God has shut me down and stopped me from having children. It is God who has blocked my way, and God is denying me." When impatience rules, people will not hesitate to blame God for what is wrong or for what is lacking in their lives.

Sarai thought she had found the answer to their problems, but it was the devil. The devil was working that timetable in their minds, and then he had a detour waiting in the wings. He had a ready-made substitute. The great Abram was very willing to obey his wife, which tells us that he was not perfect after all.

> So after Abram had been living in Canaan ten years,
> Sarai his wife took her Egyptian slave Hagar and

gave her to her husband to be his wife. He slept with
Hagar, and she conceived.

— Genesis 16:3–4 (NIV)

Guess what? It worked. They outsmarted God. *Or so they
thought.* Hagar went from slave to wife. That is what the devil
does with the counterfeits in our life. He convinces us to elevate
them to a position of importance. When people turn away from
God's path, they tend to equate the counterfeit with the blessings
of God.

But this plan did not turn out like she wanted it to. It never
does. Anytime we try to bypass God's word and God's will and
do our own thing, it turns out bad. Sooner or later, the counterfeit
will show its true colors. And it will not be what people thought
it was.

The pregnant Hagar despised Sarai. She treated her with
contempt. There is a deeper meaning in Hebrew, which speaks
about cursing. Sarai, in turn, attacks Abram and blames him for
the mess. I surmise Sarai makes her life unbearable, so Hagar
flees. But God sends her right back to them. What a mess Abram
and Sarai created for themselves. It started with a delay that they
thought they could beat. But it just went from bad to worse. The
thing they started, they could not control it, and they got so far
off track from what God promised them.

It seemed like it was all over, but God was not done with
them.

Now the LORD was gracious to Sarah as he had
said, and the LORD did for Sarah what he had
promised. Sarah became pregnant and bore a son to
Abraham in his old age, at the very time God had

promised him. Abraham was a hundred years old
when his son Isaac was born to him.

— Genesis 21:1–2, 5 (NIV)

God fulfilled His promise to Abraham. God changed their names, and God gave them a son. His name was Isaac, which means "laughter." God can turn our sorrow into joy. What an amazing God we serve.

They thought God blocked their way, but He had a miracle in the making all the time. Despite the mess they created with Hagar, God did not give up on them. Isaac was God's plan. But he was more. Isaac was God's original plan for them.

"Original" means "initial, fundamental, primary, and first." "Original" means "the thing that God wanted to do in you and for you and through you from even before you were born." That is the thing that the devil fights the hardest—the original plan. His goal is for us to settle for the lesser plan, for the substitute or the counterfeit.

God gave Abraham and Sarah their original plan after they took a detour. God gave Abraham and Sarah their original plan after they were sidetracked and settled for a substitute. It was quite a mess they created. All of them were in it together. Abraham was just as guilty as Sarah, and Hagar knew what she was doing too.

When it seemed like they had messed up everything and that they had gone too far, God brought through the original plan. God's original plan for you and me is still on the table. God has not changed His mind about you. God has not given up on His purpose for you.

God did not give up on Jonah. Jonah went in the opposite direction and ended up in a fish, but God never gave up on him.

God came for him. God did not give up on Peter, even after Peter denied Jesus three times. Peter had quit the ministry and went back to fishing, but Jesus came for him. The Bible is filled with such examples.

You may think that you missed your time. But I come to remind you that we belong to a God who is outside of time and space and who says that He will restore the years that were stolen from us. God is here for you and me. It is not too late for God to fulfill your original purpose today. Abraham was a hundred years old!

Don't quit on God. Don't find an alternative. Don't settle for second best. Have faith in God. What God did for Abraham and Sarah, God can do for us this year. God's original plan for you is still on the table.

Stolen

Despite whatever the devil took from you, whatever you lost, or whatever you gave up or sacrificed for the detour, God's original plan for you is still on the table.

Sabotage

Some of you have had the devil sabotage God's plan for you. He's walked all over you and did a lot of damage. You may think it's too late. God's original plan for you is still on the table.

Setbacks

Some of you have had one setback after another. It seems like one step forward and two steps backward. And maybe you think that you will never get to where you should be. God's original plan for you is still on the table.

Set Up

Some of you have been set up. People came into your life, and they looked, sounded, and acted like a gift from God. But they were really satanic representatives, and they may have done a number on you. God's original plan for you is still on the table.

Despite what the devil ruined or messed up in your life, despite what has been delayed, detoured, damaged, or derailed, God's original plan for you is still on the table. God's original purpose for our lives can still happen. If you want it, God's waiting for you.

It seems like the whole world was detoured in 2020. The whole planet went through a tough time with lots of loss, pain, and suffering. It was an unending season of fear and stress and so much chaos and confusion.

I decree and declare in the name of the Father, Son, and Holy Spirit.

What God wanted to do for you can still be done. What God had for you can still be yours. What you should have done, you can still do that. The first prophecy over your life can still be fulfilled; it has not expired. The God-given dreams, visions, and goals can still come to pass.

God is restoring minds and thinking. God is restoring wisdom, understanding, revelation, and discernment. God is healing damages that happened to our emotions and healing hurts that ruined our happiness. God can restore our health and our finances. God is turning family battlezones into loving and healthy places.

I am not finished because God is not finished with me. God's original plan for you and me is still on the table. Name the area of your life that has been detoured or delayed by the devil, and know that God can fix it.

I do not just want back what the enemy stole; I don't just want restoration; I want God's original plan and purpose for my life, and then I want some more. I want my destiny back. I want God's original plan for my life to be fulfilled. Nothing's impossible, and impossible is nothing for God. I want those blessings that rightfully belong to me because of Jesus' blood. I want those blessings with my name on them. I want those people God sent into my life that the devil ambushed. I want to preach the sermons that God wanted me to preach that I never did. I want to sing the songs that God wanted me to. I want the joy, peace, and strength that is rightfully mine in Jesus Christ.

The detour does not have to be the end of your story. Despite the level of destruction or damage, despite the depth of setbacks and failures, God's original plan for us is still on the table, so we can still be who God wants us to be. We can still have what God wants us to have. We can still do what God wants us to do. I am not finished because God is not finished with me. We may not look like we should, but God's original plan for us is still on the table.

When God gives us a promise and a purpose and plan for our lives, it rarely comes with a stopwatch or timer. I don't even think it comes with a timetable or a calendar. More often than not, I think it comes with a compass. God says, "Follow Me, and it will happen." So we go in God's direction with hope and faith that if God said it, He can and will do it.

Here is a suggestion. Write down what Satan stole, delayed, damaged, or destroyed in your life. Believe that God can give it back to you and then much more. Pray over it. You don't have to do this, but if you are comfortable, share that list with a prayer partner.

We are no ordinary prey. We do not have to let the detour be the destination of our lives. God's original plan can be ours today.

CHAPTER THIRTEEN
You're Better than Your Defeat

I have had so many defeats in my life. I have been knocked down as a wild, reckless teenager and then as a saved, Spirit-filled person. And I have had a bunch of defeats even as a pastor (*shhh…don't tell*).

Some of the things that defeated me took me by surprise. That is because the thing that knocked me back was something that I had overcome a long time ago. The devil is cunning, and he will come at us, even with things that we overcame in the past.

Have you noticed how he attacks us after we have had great victories? There have been times over the years that I have gone from the mountain top of preaching a powerful Sunday sermon down into a valley even before lunch. *I am sure many pastors know exactly what I mean.*

Some of the things that defeated me were so trivial. I have had moments of being so angry or frustrated over the silliest things. I have found myself getting worked up over things that don't really matter. And that causes me to be disappointed with myself. I remember a day that I got so angry at a driver who took too long to make a turn, and that caused me to miss the green light at a place where the traffic light takes a very long time to change. I shouted ugly things about that person. The only one who could hear me was me. It took me a few moments to reset, but I was so disappointed with my reaction. I was having a wonderful day. I had a great morning in prayer and worship. I seem to remember that we were in a season of fasting too. It took a few seconds for me to lose the blessing of that morning.

There have been moments when I said to myself, *I thought I was better than this*. And that is a powerful truth—I am better than the things that defeated me. I am no ordinary prey; I should not have stumbled or tripped over that situation or challenge. In such moments, I took my walk with God for granted. In those times, I was living off yesterday's victories. We simply cannot let our guard down. This is a daily walk with God, and we have to always be ready for the call to the battlefield.

Israel entered the promised land under Joshua's leadership. There was an established pattern to their lives during the forty years in the wilderness. But as they stepped into the promised land, God brought some radical changes—He was taking away the cloud and the fire pillar that were over them every single day of their journey. The miraculous free food, manna, was also going away. And then, to top it all, the only leader they knew, Moses, had died. They were stepping into the unknown with a bunch of radical changes. It was a frightening moment.

Their first order of business was to take the city of Jericho. Israel marched around their walls once a day for six days and seven times on the seventh day. The walls fell just as God said they would. Then they went on to the next assignment, the city of Ai. Joshua sent over spies who came back with a very encouraging report.

> When they returned to Joshua, they said, "Not all the army will have to go up against Ai. Send two or three thousand men to take it and do not weary the whole army, for only a few people live there."
> — Joshua 7:3 (NIV)

"The spies say there are a few people, so we don't need to send everyone, just send a few people. This is not Jericho. We don't need the A team, the marines, or the navy seals. Don't send all the Avengers. No need to bother everyone." Fresh from the victory at Jericho, Joshua and the people must have been so pumped up. Obviously, Joshua loved this report, and he took their advice.

> So about three thousand went up; but they were
> routed by the men of Ai.
>
> — Joshua 7:4 (NIV)

But something went wrong. A city far smaller than Jericho put them to flight. A city less powerful than Jericho took them down. They fled with their tails between their legs.

> Who killed about thirty-six of them. They chased
> the Israelites from the city gate as far as the stone
> quarries and struck them down on the slopes. At
> this the hearts of the people melted in fear and
> became like water.
>
> — Joshua 7:5 (NIV)

They lost thirty-six people. It rattled them and shattered their bravado. Their confidence was broken. The Hebrew word *macac* means "to dissolve, melt." It means "to waste away, faint, and grow fearful." This was no ordinary fear. It was a fear for their lives. It was a permeating fear that saturated every part of their existence. If you have ever been afraid, then you know it can be overwhelming. Their hearts were melting and their courage dissolving. Israel was getting weaker every moment.

They had just crushed Jericho but got defeated by a far weaker enemy. They went from the mountain top to the valley. Joshua cries out to the Lord. The reason for their defeat was Achan, who stole from Jericho in disobedience to the Lord.

> The LORD said to Joshua, "Stand up! What are you doing down on your face? Israel has sinned; they have violated my covenant, which I commanded them to keep. They have taken some of the devoted things; they have stolen, they have lied, they have put them with their own possessions. That is why the Israelites cannot stand against their enemies; they turn their backs and run because they have been made liable to destruction. I will not be with you anymore unless you destroy whatever among you is devoted to destruction."
>
> — Joshua 7:10–12 (NIV)

God said to Joshua that Israel was the reason for their defeat. God told him to get off his face, stand up, and go fix it. The Hebrew word is *quwm*. That means "to arise or stand up." There is more to this word. It also means "to arise" in a hostile sense, to arise and become powerful.

These were God's instructions, "Go and identify the problem." When we pray, the Holy Spirit will help us identify the gaps. When we identify the issues, then we can deal with them. We have to be able to put a name on it.

It's easy to blame others or the devil for our problems. Some people even blame the Lord. It takes courage to say, "Lord, it's my fault." It takes courage to confess and repent. It takes courage to be humble before God. We cannot be sorry for what we refuse to acknowledge even exists. If we can address the inside issues, then no matter what happens on the outside, we will be fine. If we can be good with God on the inside, then it does not matter what people may say about us or do against us. That is why the devil could not destroy Daniel. Because Daniel had determined in his heart not to defile himself. That is why the devil could not destroy Shadrach, Meshach, and Abednego: because they refused to bow to the idol, whether God saved them or not. That is why the devil could not destroy Job: because Job's declaration was, "Even if God kills me, I trust Him."

The name of the city of Ai in Hebrew means "a heap of ruins." The thing that defeated them was not such a big deal. Israel could have defeated them with a handful of people. Israel could have destroyed them even if their soldiers had one hand tied behind their backs.

The same applies to us. There are battles that we should have never lost. Samson should have never surrendered to Delilah. Elijah should have never run from Jezebel. Abraham should have never said yes to the Hagar option.

The devil will take any gap he can get. John 10:10 warns us that the devil comes into our lives to steal, kill, and destroy.

If you look back, you may be embarrassed at the things that defeated you because you were better than that. You are better than the thing that knocked you down. You are better than your issues. You are better than your weaknesses. You are better than your failures. When we work on the inside, God will give us the victory that we should have had.

The essence of Christianity is the power to change, so we don't have to be the same. It is power, so you don't have to stay in the place you are in. And we definitely don't have to stay in defeat. It begins with a choice. *I am not going to stay down. I am going to get back up and fight again.*

You may have been defeated in the past, but you are no longer the same person. Israel was no longer in the wilderness; they were in the promised land. They had come through much, and they made it so far by the grace of God. And God had more for them. They faced a choice—wallow in defeat or try again.

You have to make up your mind. *I am not going back to who I used to be. I am not going back to where I used to be. I am not going back to the people I used to be with. I am not going back to the words I used to speak. I am not going back to the attitudes or the sinful habits.* When you make up your mind that you are not going back, it changes what God does on your behalf. It changes what the enemy can do against you.

When you come through tough stuff, you cannot go back. When you survive, you cannot go back to who you used to be. When you break loose from the things that should have killed you or destroyed you, you cannot go back. So we have to make up our minds. *I came too far to go back. I suffered too much to go back now. I cried too many tears to go back now. I had too much pain to go back now. I lost too many precious moments; I lost too many precious relationships to go back now. I lost too many destiny opportunities; I lost too many divine moments to go back now. I refuse to be who I used to be; I refuse to do what I used to do. I will not return to the chains; I will not return to the bondages or addictions. I will not go back to the confusion and chaos. I will not be that person again.*

If you have been defeated, know this; you deserve a better life because of what God did for you on the cross. God is looking for people who are committed to changing their lives. God is looking for someone who will dig their heels and face any challenge because they want to move forward. Some people give up too soon because they got knocked down. People quit because they see no way ahead.

My grandfather had a favorite song, "When I Remember What the Lord Has Done." It is an old South African song. I could not find the name of the original artist. Some of the words are:

When I remember what the Lord has done
I'll never go back anymore
No No No No No
I'll never go back anymore

There are too many people who make wonderful progress only to quit because of a setback. God wants us to step fully into the next level that He has for us. Don't miss the next steps that God has for you. Don't miss the open doors. Don't miss the miracles ahead of you. Don't miss the new things God wants to do for you. God is ready to help those who make up their minds that they will not give up. We are no ordinary prey. We may be knocked down, but we refuse to stay down.

We are no ordinary prey. Don't judge me by what has knocked me down because I have a God, and He can take me beyond this level. We are no ordinary prey. Don't judge me by what I have or where I am because I have a God, and He can take me beyond this defeat. We are no ordinary prey. I may be running on empty, but don't write me off. We are no ordinary prey. I may be in a mess or a desperate place, but don't count me out because I have a God, and He can take me beyond this level. I have a God, and I am looking to Him. We are no ordinary prey.

Have you noticed how the moment you start to progress in your walk with God, you come up against some opposition? Depending on how strong your resolve is, that is the strength of the attack that will come against you. The devil will pay little attention to someone who is no threat to him and his operation. But the moment you start to pray with some passion and power, expect the enemy to take notice of you. The moment you start reading the Bible and having serious devotions, expect Satan to try to disrupt you. The moment you start giving and tithing, expect Satan to come against you with lies. The moment you decide, "I am going to follow Jesus," expect demonic attacks against your faith.

It is when you start moving forward with God that Satan will try to shut you down. It is when you start to make progress that he will want to shut you up, steal your passion, or knock you off balance. The intention is to stop people from following through with what they have started. The biggest challenge most of us face is what we will do after we have been knocked down. It begins with a choice, "I am not going to stay down. I am going to get back up and fight again."

The small thing that knocked you down does not have to be your swan song. I have said this countless times to our congregation, "A defeat does not have to be the end of one's story. It does not have to be your final chapter." The Israel that took down the powerful Jericho was restored. And they were able to fight again.

The person you used to be can be restored. The anointing you used to have can be restored. You can still be the one God is looking for. You can still be who you wanted to be. You can still be what others thought you were. You can still be what God said you could be.

Concluding Note

Joshua cries out to God after their defeat. God's reply can be summarized like this, "Joshua, they did not defeat you; you defeated yourself." Anyone can have a fail point. But everyone has access to God's grace point because of the blood of Jesus. And it all begins with faith point. If you are willing, the Holy Spirit will help you work on your issues and help you be the better person you were meant to be.

Prophetic Declarations

I prophetically declare in Jesus' name, "The best is yet to come." I prophetically declare that the best blessings are still ahead of you. I prophetically declare that the best relationships and friendships are still ahead of you. I prophetically declare that the best revelations, teachings, preaching, and serving are yet to be. I prophetically declare that the greatest testimonies and miracles are still ahead of you. I prophetically declare that your best days and your blessed days are ahead of you. Praise God for the past. The best is yet to come. So get up and fight again.

I am believing that the greatest blessing that I am going to be is still to happen. The greatest sermon that I am going to preach is yet to happen. My most amazing experience in the Holy Spirit is still to come. I can be more effective and relevant than I have ever been. I can touch more lives than I have ever done before. My best singing has not yet taken place. My greatest moments in God have not yet happened because there is more that God has for me. And I declare the same for you.

CONCLUSION

No ordinary prey! That is who we are. No ordinary prey means that we are not powerless victims. No ordinary prey means we are mighty through our God. No ordinary prey means that we respond with the weapons God gave us against whatever the devil does or tries to do against us.

No ordinary prey is not passive. No ordinary prey is not pessimistic. No ordinary prey is not easily put off. No ordinary prey does not give in to frustration or delays. No ordinary prey means we fight with all we have. No ordinary prey means never ever accept defeat by the devil.

We are no ordinary prey. And we are never alone in the battle. Our God is with us in the battle. We are not alone because there is an army of God all over the world taking the fight to the powers of darkness.

Thank you for taking the time to read this book. I hope that your faith was stirred up and that your desire to fight the good fight of faith was renewed. I pray that you will become all that God created and called you to be—a mighty kingdom-of-God warrior on the earth.

Blessings.

EPILOGUE

I have walked that long road to freedom. I have tried
not to falter; I have made missteps along the way.
But I have discovered the secret that after climbing
a great hill, one only finds that there are many more
hills to climb. I have taken a moment here to rest,
to steal a view of the glorious vista that surrounds
me, to look back on the distance I have come. But I
can only rest for a moment, for with freedom comes
responsibilities, and I dare not linger, for my long
walk is not ended.

That quote from President Nelson Mandela wonderfully captures
this way of life. We are no ordinary prey. But we must know that
after a victory, there will be another battle waiting for us. After praying through the victory in one challenge, there will be
a bunch of other urgent prayer requests in our inbox. After our
praises put the devil to flight, there will be more battle songs that
need to be vocalized, most likely in dark, deep valleys.

We celebrate our victories. Hallelujah! But we know that as
long as we are on the earth, we are engaged in an ongoing spiritual warfare against a relentless enemy. We have to keep fighting.
We are no ordinary prey, and through our God, we will go from
victory to victory.

BIBLIOGRAPHY

Mandela, Nelson. *Long Walk to Freedom*. London: Abacus, 1995.

The Holy Bible, New International Version (NIV). Copyright © 1973, 1978, 1984, 2011 by Biblica, Inc.™ Used by permission. All rights reserved worldwide.

ABOUT THE AUTHOR

Nelson Naicker is married to Valerie. They have a daughter, Kimberly, a son-in-law, Sean, and a son, Jordan.

Nelson Naicker was born and raised in South Africa. He graduated from the Bethesda Bible College. He obtained his Master of Divinity degree from the Church of God Theological Seminary in Cleveland, Tennessee. And he got his Doctor of Ministry degree from Asbury Theological Seminary in Wilmore, Kentucky. His doctorate was part of the Beeson Pastor Program.

Prior to moving to the United States, he pastored the Nazareth Full Gospel Church in Durban, South Africa. Nelson also lectured at the Bethesda Bible College in preaching and church history. He served as the denominational representative on the team of chaplains for the University of Durban-Westville.

Today, Nelson Naicker is the pastor of the El Bethel Assembly of God Church in Staten Island, New York City (www.Facebook.com/ElBethelAG).

CPSIA information can be obtained
at www.ICGtesting.com
Printed in the USA
LVHW020018250622
721982LV00012B/232